DAWN L. CRUMBLE

Until Something Happens

Waiting for the Manifestation of Your Prayers

By

Dawn L. Crumble

Copyright © 2023 by Dawn L. Crumble
Soaring Beyond, an imprint of Winged Publications

All rights reserved. Non-commercial interests may reproduce portions of this book without the express written permission of the authors, provided the text does not exceed 500 words.

Commercial interests: No part of this publication may be reproduced in any form, stored in a retrieval system, or transmitted in any form by any means—electronic, photocopy, recording, or otherwise—except as provided by the United States of America copyright law.

Author represented by AuthorizeMe Literary Firm LLC
Sharon Norris Elliott, Agent
PO Box 1816, South Gate, CA 90280
www.AuthorizeMe.net
AuthorizeMeNow@gmail.com

Scriptures are taken from the New King James Version®. Copyright © 1982 by Thomas Nelson. Used by permission. All rights reserved.

The Amplified Bible. Copyright ©1954, 1958, 1962, 1964, 1965, 1987 by The Lockman Foundation. All rights reserved. Used by permission. Published by Zondervan. Grand Rapids, Michigan 49530, U.S.A.

Cover photo by Cornel Randolph

All rights reserved.
ISBN: 978-1-0881-6261-3

What Others Are Saying

Pastor Dawn has delivered a phenomenal book that promises to inspire those called to intercessory prayer. The reader is invited on a journey to pursue an intimate relationship with God as she gives us a glimpse into her own personal journey. Be prepared to laugh, cry, and be imparted revelation as Pastor Dawn teaches you what to do Until Something Happens!
Dr. Shanicka N. Scarbrough, MD
Her Testimony Ministries and author of
Power to Heal Your Heart

This is not another book written to women but instead is written to be a journey together with Dawn Crumble in overcoming silent pain towards healing in an adventure of prayer. Join Dawn to live in the forgiveness God offers in a conversational relationship with Him that speaks life into dry bones.
Dr. Mark Dahlin
Biblical Studies Department Chair
and Professor of Spiritual Formation
Epic Bible College and Graduate School of Theology

Do you need encouragement while you are waiting? While you are waiting on God to manifest the prayers you have been praying, it is important to invest in tools that assist you in the process. Everything in our lives is hinged on our ability to pray to a God who hears us and believes that in His divine timing, through pain, setbacks, trauma, and victories, God will bring us through, and our prayers will be answered. Seasons change, life changes, turbulence occurs and if we don't faint, victory shows up as answered prayers. We can see that the hand of God was always working on our behalf. For any person feeling like waiting is in vain or you are just tired of waiting, allow this book by Dawn Crumble to ignite your ability to wait well. Until Something Happens is sure to bless you in a major way to never stop believing, hoping, and standing on His promises for your life.

Dana D. Mizell
Dana Berry Ministries
Southfield, Michigan

Intercessor Dawn Crumble is a True God Send to The Body of Christ. Intercessor Dawn Crumble illustrates in this book how God calls an intercessor, how an intercessor speaks to God, hears from God, and prays with the Power of God. Intercessor Dawn Crumble has been called by God from an early age, has truly answered the call, and is walking with power in the calling. Intercessor Dawn Crumble opens up about her true-life experiences, how God has impacted her life, her ministry, and the lives of those around her. Until Something Happens will benefit all who read this book, especially those seeking to learn more about the life of an intercessor. I recommend Until Something Happens as a deepened read for readers across denominational lines, cultures, and of all ages, a must-have.

> Sr. Pastor T.R. Harris. Senior Pastor of New Life Christian Fellowship Center Texas
> Master Of Arts in Religion in Pastoral Ministry
> Graduate of Liberty University Baptist Theological Seminary and The Helms School of Government

For years, the church has struggled with the challenge of how to minister to women and couples who have chosen to have an abortion. In this reading, the author gives the readers a ministerial type of blueprint on how one can navigate through the post-abortion syndrome struggles of suicidal thoughts, depression, pains, and regrets.

Through the author's transparency, the reader can see how one's sin and wounds can become a calling to bring healing and salvation to others. This book gives biblical principles to recover from sins in life, establish physical strength to get up after years of pain and be healed from the trauma that many hurting women go through. It is evident that Dawn Crumble was wounded enough to bring salvation to others.

As the Bible teaches, "Jesus was wounded for our transgressions, he was bruised for our iniquities, the chastisement of our peace was upon him, and with his stripes we are healed." Isiah 53:5-8 KJV. As they read this book, people will experience an impartation of God's power of forgiveness, deliverance, and healing, and be made whole. This is a must-read for people who are living with post-abortion syndrome issues.

    Henry Pigee, Pastor and Founder
    Church of the Word Ministries/The Word Center Ministries
    President of HPPI Prophetic Institute
    Presiding Prelate of Prophetic International Fellowship

Table of Contents

What Others Are Saying
Error! Bookmark not defined.

Contents
Error! Bookmark not defined.

My Tribute and Dedication
Error! Bookmark not defined.

Acknowledgments
Error! Bookmark not defined.

My Prayer for You
Error! Bookmark not defined.

Foreword
Error! Bookmark not defined.

Chapter 1
Error! Bookmark not defined.

Chapter 2
Error! Bookmark not defined.

Chapter 3
Error! Bookmark not defined.

Chapter 4
Error! Bookmark not defined.

Chapter 5
Error! Bookmark not defined.

Chapter 6
Error! Bookmark not defined.

Chapter 7
Error! Bookmark not defined.

Chapter 8
Error! Bookmark not defined.

Chapter 9
Error! Bookmark not defined.

Chapter 10
Error! Bookmark not defined.

Chapter 11
Error! Bookmark not defined.

Chapter 12
Error! Bookmark not defined.

Chapter 13
Error! Bookmark not defined.

Chapter 14
Error! Bookmark not defined.

About the Author **Error! Bookmark not defined.**

UNTIL SOMETHING HAPPENS

My Tribute and Dedication

I could not have come up with a book like this without a complete vision from God Almighty, inspiration from my Lord Jesus the Christ, and leading from Holy Spirit. My life is much better for Your presence, and I have decided Your plan is the best and I am eternally grateful.

My first prayer partners were my maternal grandparents, Moses and Allie Crumble. God gave me an excellent foundation. I will see you again.

The years 1995 and 1999 are my favorites. God blessed me with two amazing, beautiful daughters. You make me laugh, dance, rejoice, and proud to be your mum. Thank you for teaching me, learning with me, and loving me just the way I am.

Acknowledgments

I acknowledge my parents, Marvin and Patricia Guillory, who taught me how to survive the hard parts of life. My handsome brother, Ku Crumble, I am so glad you are my one and only.

I acknowledge the Women Who Pray Ministries, you are an amazing group of praying sisters. I thank my God for you daily and for this assignment He has entrusted me since before the foundation of the world. Let's keep praying bold prayers together.

I acknowledge the many women who made, taught, and encouraged me to pray and challenged me to study and exhort the Word. You know who you are. Without you and the Lord on my side, where would I be? Thank you for your shoulders which I stand on humbly.

And finally, to everyone who prayed for me during this project, purchased an advance copy, checked in, and pushed me, thank you. I am grateful for your love and constant support.

My Prayer for You

Father in Heaven, I stand praying for the one who has purchased Until Something Happens or has received it as a gift, that Father will bless them richly with every spiritual gift. I stand in prayer that their faith will be strengthened and stretched in You. I stand in prayer that they will come to know You through praying in a more intimate way. I stand praying that they will develop prayer muscles, their faith will grow feet, and that they are desperate enough to seek You daily. This I stand praying in the mighty and matchless name of my Lord Jesus the Christ and it is sealed with the blood of the Lamb. Amen

Foreword

Prayer is our main form of communication with the Father. When we pray, we seek answers, and often the lack of answers in prayer gives way to aborting what has been requested from the Lord. How many times have you prayed, sought answers or fulfillment, and subconsciously put a time limit on your faith for that very prayer? How many times have you prayed without any expectation due to not consistently receiving an answer in your time frame? The answer to these questions may vary but they are indeed an introspective task. In reading this manuscript, I have been overwhelmed by its vibrant message and the need to encourage all who are called to be prayer warriors, intercessors, and for others who are seeking instructions on what to do while waiting for God to answer their prayers.

I met Pastor Dawn Crumble during a Friday night service in Texas. We were both invited to be on the program for that event. Her assignment was to give encouraging words and pray through the Holy Spirit throughout the service. There were many gifts on the program, but it was through her prayer that she articulated the pulse, heartbeat, and the breath of God during that service. It was evident that this was not just a task for her, this is her lifestyle. It was also clear why she was chosen for this time. Her access to the Father allowed these doors to be open.

Take note that while reading Until Something Happens, you will be empowered with what to do while you are waiting for the Lord to manifest His will. It will equip you with the necessary tools to be consistent in your prayer life and walk with Christ. No matter how many times you read this book, you will be encouraged to seek God and develop an authentic relationship with the Father through prayer. This will also rekindle the key elements necessary to receive while waiting on God. Without hesitation, Pastor Crumble exposes the defects and cliches that cause people to stop praying when there is no light in sight.

Pastor Crumble's writing is practical with biblical principles to follow. As you read each section, you can feel her passion for prayer which is the heart and life of her ministry. I encourage you to read this life-changing book. This uplifting and instructional book will help you navigate those unsure moments in your prayer life. It will also empower you to make the proper changes chapter by chapter. Permit it to influence you to live a lifestyle of prayer that will nurture you as you pray until something happens.

Bishop G.F. Henfield
Pastor, Family Empowerment Center
Valdosta, Georgia

DAWN L. CRUMBLE

DAWN L. CRUMBLE

Chapter 1
In The Beginning

Our story began in 1986. I remember the day he and I met all too vividly. He was a customer who visited my job often—tall, caramel, with a smile and eyes that had me immediately hooked. One day, he came in with Debra's Special cookies from Mrs. Fields. He offered, but I declined.

"I like semi-sweet with nuts," I said.

Off he went, back to Mrs. Fields to get me what I wanted. Somewhere along the course of his frequent visits, we finally exchanged phone numbers, and then we had our first date. I found myself in his arms and then his kiss. Oh, yes, I was definitely hooked. And the rest? Well, it goes like this….

In complete disbelief of what was happening, I wondered, how could this be? The test was positive. He said he loved me, and I said I loved him. After all, we had been together for two years. This should not be a decision of what to do, but an announcement of celebration. We were not kids and yet that is exactly what I felt like—a little girl not knowing what to do. I saw our baby as someone I would finally have to love me unconditionally and someone I could love without reservation. The baby would be someone to call my own. I was ready to make the grand announcement. I had it all planned out. My mother first, then his father, and reluctantly, we would have to tell his mother. Yeah, I had it all planned. I was excited. Me, the man of my dreams, and our baby made from love.

To my surprise, I was pregnant with not just one baby, but with twins. I felt an urgency to name them Brandon Lamar and Bethany Joy. The more parenthood stared me in the face, the more I said their names, the more excited I became. Sadly, our twins' father did not feel the same way. He felt we needed to make a decision. A decision about what? My decision was clear. I was going to be a mother, he was going to be a father, and I did not want to parent alone. These twins had parents, and we needed to face this together.

A month passed with every bit of continued shock and uncertainty, and still we had not made our announcement. I began wondering, "What am I doing?" Constant concerns that swirled in my mind were endless. "What will my mother say? How will her church friends react?" Having grown up in church, I knew a pregnant unmarried woman was taboo and looked down upon. It would bring shame, and my life would forever be darkened. What would my neighbors think? I was a good girl but had seriously missed the target of marriage, then baby. Nevertheless, here I was pregnant, single, and devastated.

I had begun showing and I was glad about my tiny but defined baby bump. The days and weeks drew closer to the day of no turning back. We made the decision, or rather he made the decision, that having the child would make our lives too complicated. I bought the lie that we would be a happily-ever-after couple if it remained just the two of us, so we set the appointment for the abortion.

To my surprise, the abortion clinic was not what I expected. It was clean and resembled an upscale medical office. The staff confirmed the pregnancy with a quick examination and scheduled the procedure. The reality was setting in. I had made the biggest, horrific decision of my life—to end the lives of my twins.

The week leading up to the appointment seemed like an eternity. When the day finally arrived, I was a ball of wild nervousness. The anxiety about everything that would follow had me terrified of the result. I remember lying on the table, trying to make candid conversation with the doctor to stretch the time with every excuse. Finally, the general anesthesia was administered, and tears streamed down my face. I asked my twins and God to forgive me. Hearing the screams of the other women, I fell asleep. When I awakened, it was over. A pool of blood was left behind me and no more twins.

Twins' father and I had our grieving moments. For him, it was only a moment. For me, it would take months to stop the tears. The ability to go around babies or attend baby showers was nearly impossible. I could still hear the screams of the other women in the clinic. The abdominal pains were an overwhelming reminder of what I had done, and the mental anguish was crushing and bottled up tightly within me. There was no one I could tell. Who would understand? Twins' father had failed me, so being alone and lonely was my new everyday norm. I had never been to this place before; it was unfamiliar, hard, and embarrassing. While no one knew, I knew, twins' father knew, and I was fully aware that God knew too.

Sinking into depression, thoughts of suicide consumed me. Grief and shame were my clothing. This would go on far too long. I wanted my twins back. I wanted desperately to reverse my actions and my decision. I had no support that I could confide in or that would understand. I had heard of other women having abortions, but I had not heard of their grief, depression, or shame. I was alone on my island. Every little girl and boy I would see brought back the painful memory and the realization that I would never see my twins. I tried sharing my feelings with a few friends but was only laughed at and ridiculed. On many occasions, I was told, "Girl, get over it and him. You deserve better. What would you do with twins anyway?" Nobody understood the levels of pain, depression, or loneliness I was struggling with. Nobody.

Two years passed and the moment finally came when I knew within myself it was time for me to get up. I had to pull myself up because no one would help me. I had to move on from the most painful experience of my life. An elderly gentleman questioned me, "Have you gone to church?"

I tried coming up with every excuse not to go, but he always had a comeback question or resolution. The excuses escaped me, so one Sunday I found my way to church. That day, I rededicated my life to God by accepting the Lord Jesus as my Savior. Unfortunately, it did not change my immediate feelings of depression or my memory. The church was full of families who had the cutest kids, and none were mine.

I found myself teaching the kindergarten Sunday school class. I agreed to this post for my selfish reasons: to be around what I once had and wanted so badly. To my surprise, my healing began with those little ones. The biggest hugs and smiles came from the smallest faces. My lap was always overcrowded, but I loved every minute of it. Sunday was my favorite day and spending that hour with them was my greatest place of restoration. Throughout this healing journey, my Sunday school class became my safe place—a place of deliverance and comfort, even though it was also a place of pain. But even in that pain, being with the little ones brought a missed smile to my face and added laughter to my voice.

As I progressed in my walk with God and in my healing, my relationship with the twins' father was no longer the same. While I desired to hold on to him, our relationship was strained and distant. It simply was not God's plan for my life. It was over between us, so now my healing was not only about my twins, but it was also about getting over him as well. I had become less desirable to him.

Thankfully, growing in prayer was the answer I desperately needed.

Over a two-year-long healing process, much happened, and I never thought being called into ministry would be on that list...but his forgiveness came with a price It was the price of my surrendering to God. I remember hearing clearly, "Will you pray for my people"? And just like that, while I did not give birth physically, God allowed me to birth a ministry for hurting women. In my pain, God decided I was still valuable, and He had some women who needed rescuing, healing, and restoring. With my resounding yes to God, I asked Him to show me and tell me about these hurting women.

Are you a woman who needs healing? God allows me to feel your pain, your hurt, your brokenness, and your point of desperation and loneliness. I am with you in your journey from brokenness to wholeness. I am with you to listen and undergird you. I am with you through the process of restoration. You have more than what it takes to survive. You have what it takes to thrive. God made you beautiful, strong, loving, and resilient. And in your restoration, forgive those who hurt you, and most importantly, forgive yourself. God has.

And My Story Continues

As a little girl living with my maternal grandparents in Milwaukee, prayer was my foundation. I learned to pray by watching and listening. Praying was the first act of our mornings and prayer finished our evenings. I joined my grandparents on my knees by their bedside with my little hands folded as we read the Holy Scriptures and recited the Lord's Prayer. My goal was to have them one day join me by my bedside for reading and evening prayer. I believe they would be proud of me now as much as I was excited to learn from them as a young child. I remember my first powerful ah-ha prayer moment like it was yesterday.

From the age of three, I was left in the care of my maternal grandparents while my mother moved to California to get established as a young woman and start her life. As the years passed, I became known as the little girl who helped set the communion table and get the new converts ready for baptism. God had begun ordering my footsteps.

One day, I overheard my grandmothers (maternal and paternal) having a conversation about me. Standing in the doorway listening to their conversation, I heard, "You have raised her for seven years, now let me have her for the next seven. She is my granddaughter too."

Imagine me watching as a seven-year-old child, watching with my eyes moving back and forth and listening while my ears tuned in for my life's fate. Would my grandmother agree to let me live with my other grandmother with whom I barely had a relationship? What would happen to my everyday life? Would I go to church on Sunday? Would there be any more prayer time?

The grandmother I lived with was calm but

stern. "Let me pray about it. Come back next week. I will have an answer."

The room was quiet and surprisingly my other grandmother complied. What a powerful statement, "Let me pray about it." *What exactly does that mean,* I wondered? *What is the outcome after prayer? How can one statement change the trajectory of a situation?* I would soon find out.

Let Me Pray About It

I knew immediately at the young age of seven I wanted to be able to say, "Let me pray about it," and people would agree with me. I clearly remember the feeling of abandonment: my mother moved away, my father was not present in my life, and my maternal grandfather was insistent on sending me to California to be with my mother. At that moment, and at many more to follow, I became familiar with the idea "let me pray about it." My grandmother talked to God every day and sometimes several times a day. It was what she did and what she taught me to do.

One week later my paternal grandmother returned to our home for the God-sent answer.

"No, she needs to be in California with her mother," declared my grandmother.

At that moment, I knew there was something special about prayer, and I wanted that kind of authority and power that grabbed the attention of others and held them captive until God had given His answer. The phrase "let me pray about it" would forever be ingrained in my mind. Prayer had just become interesting to my seven-year-old self.

Moving to California, attending church

regularly was now a thing of the past. I would not attend church again until I was twelve, though not regularly. I walked to the neighborhood Catholic church. To me, it was a church, and I could participate in holy communion. It was not the same as I was accustomed to, but the foundation had been laid and prayer had become very much a part of my DNA. If I did not know anything else, I knew that attending church regularly and praying was the answer to my problems. I thought prayer was the norm for everyone. And strangely, I thought everyone had a prayer foundation too.

By attending church regularly and the solidity of my prayer life, I often even prayed in the shower. I was not a timely person and often ran fifteen minutes behind, so, in my wisdom, I decided I would kill two birds with one stone. Shower and pray, pray and shower. And wouldn't you know it, there would be mornings when I would pray until the water was ice cold, and I still ended up late for work. During those ice-cold prayer times, I would find myself basking in the presence of the Lord. It was as if God and I were both waiting for our one-on-one communion time. I fell in love with my time with God, and I never got to kill those two birds. Prayer would always take priority.

Then came the dreaded season in 1989. Barely out of my teens, I messed up, was bamboozled by the devil, and found myself in a terrible predicament. So terrible that I stopped taking showers and started taking baths. The shower had become my prayer closet, and in my young mind, the shower was where Holy Spirit resided. But now I was taking a bath unaware that my life was about to be changed forever. The Holy Spirit visited me right in the bathtub. The water stilled to a hush.

"Why are you here in my bathtub?" I asked Holy Spirit.

"You are supposed to be in the shower."

Feeling guilt and shame, I began to weep. I wept to the point of my crying becoming ugly and uncontrollable. Never had I been told about hard conversations with God. This was new, uncomfortable, and embarrassing. I begged, "God, if you forgive me and get me out of this mess, I will do whatever you want."

There was dead silence as I continued to plead for His forgiveness. And in His still small voice, God asked me, "Will you pray for My people?

"Yes, Lord, I will pray for your people."

God asked me again, "Will you pray for My people?"

At that moment, I realized God was serious and I had better make sure I was serious too. I humbly answered, "Yes, Lord, I will pray for your people."

I had just accepted God's invitation to be His Intercessor. One prayer request after another began to come to me: pray for this, pray for that, pray for this person, pray for that person, go here to pray, go there to pray. Pray. Pray. Pray. Praying became my job. Owning up to my responsibility and the assignment I committed to sets the foundation of why I penned this book. And thirty-plus years later, my cell phone has not stopped ringing, and my inbox has never been empty of prayer requests.

The Conversations

Not fully understanding what I had said yes to, I knew I needed more spiritually—more spiritual maturity to answer that question. More training, more knowledge, more of everything, and certainly more anointing. I began praying for myself to obtain God's direction.

The Holy Spirit led me to a new church, a new denomination, and my first-ever bishop. "What in the world was I doing?" was a nagging question. After two months at First Church of God, I asked to have an appointment with the bishop. "What is a bishop? How is he different from a pastor? Will he even meet with me?" In my eyes, this bishop was a giant, not only physically, but also in his thunderous voice and even bigger presence.

The meeting was confirmed, and the day had come I would get to have a personal meeting. As I sat looking across the mahogany desk, he said, "Hello daughter, I am Bishop Reid. How can I help you?"

The conversation went on for thirty minutes. He answered all sorts of questions about himself, the church, the denomination, and women in ministry. He finally asked me, "Is there anything else you want to know?"

Holy Spirit reminded me, "You have a captive audience with the bishop. Ask the question."

Right away, I answered, "Yes, I do have another question. Why do I always have an urgency to pray?"

The bishop's answer blew me away. His posture changed. He sat up at attention with widened eyes. "It's you I have been praying for."

"Me?"

"Yes, you. You said yes to ministry."

"No, not me. I did not say yes to ministry."

"Yes, you did. In fact, you were sitting in your bathtub when you said yes."

Imagine the look on my face. This man whom I had only known for two months had just informed me what I was doing and where I was when I said yes to God. After my amazed look relaxed, Bishop Reid began to share everything he knew about the ministry of intercessory prayer, the life of an intercessor, and how to operate in that calling. Just let me say this, saying yes to God without an inkling of what you are saying yes to, is not my recommendation. You never know what God will ask you to do or what the full scope of the assignment entails. Kneeling with my grandparents in prayer was the genesis of my calling, the bathtub was the catapult, and that meeting with Bishop Reid will always have a defining place in my life.

January 2015, I recommitted to the call on my life. Recommit you ask? Yes, recommit. After a while doing the work of praying, I got tired and grew weary. It happens. I did not forsake my call, I just decreased my availability to people. After my morning devotion, I had a stern and revelatory conversation with God. It went like this:

"What do you want me to do, Lord?"

God answered rather quickly. "What are you supposed to be doing?

"Oh, you want me to still pray for your people?

"Start a prayer group."

"Well, I will need help this time, I cannot do

intercessory prayer by myself."

"What do you need?"

I concocted my to-do list for God of everything I thought I would need to operate as an intercessor and start a prayer ministry. God gently asked, "Is that all you need?"

"I do not know everything I need, but when I think of something more, I will be back. And if I am starting a prayer group, we will need a name."

"Who are you?"

"Women."

"And what will you be doing?"

"Praying."

"Well, that is who you are, Women Who Pray."

And just like that Women Who Pray was born. Seven of my friends joined me. During the following days, God clued me in on His secret. "The eight of you will never reach the hurting women that will come through Women Who Pray." The name would eventually be changed to include Ministries, as we became a spiritual triage.

As this ministry began to grow and flourish over the years, thousands of women were helped, healed, and ministered to. The Lord soon began to whisper to my spirit, "Write the book."

"What book?" My mind tried to piece together what the Lord was asking of me. What book did He want me to write?

> Finally, I heard God say, "You are thinking too hard. What is that you are called to do?" "I pray, Lord."

The Book Conversation

Pondering all the different subtopics that exist pertaining to prayer, my time with God would set the course of why there must be clarity in the waiting process connected with prayer. I was awakened in the middle of the night with a question from God. I had been in constant prayer about a situation, and I knew I had to ask and keep asking, seek and keep seeking, and knock and keep knocking (Matthew 7:7).

One evening, I heard God ask, "Now that you have prayed, what are you going to do?"

With a quick response, I answered, "pray some more."

Wondering why God would ask such a question, I was hoping I gave the right answer. God replied, "I have already answered your prayer. You are waiting for the manifestation of what I have already said yes to. What are you going to do?"

I was puzzled and began to listen for instructions. When God spoke, He shared His answer of what needs to happen between me and my praying and my prayers manifesting. I immediately got a WOW in my spirit. What a blessing to know my prayers were answered. I was waiting for the manifestation of my prayers, and there was some work I needed to do. This is when I began to understand the P-word List regarding prayer.

> Pray without ceasing.
> Prophesy to the dry bones of the situation
> Praise Him in the wait
> Press into His presence

Process your actions
Prepare for what is next
Persevere when times are rough
Pursue His will
Plan for the finish
Preach His word
Position yourself
Persist like never before
Proclaim His promises
Please Him in every deed
Practice what you are declaring, and
Pause for His direction.

No longer are we to only pray until something happens. God has given us the mandate to do the other P-words too. This knowledge set my spirit on fire for Him even more! There was so much more to my "until something happens" once I began to submit to the will of God and seek His righteousness, I knew He would surely add all these things to me (Matthew 6:33). Let's get through this PUSH—pray until something happens—together! Owning up to my responsibility and the assignment I committed to, sets the foundation of why I penned this book.

DAWN L. CRUMBLE

Chapter 2
There Is an Upset in Hell

Did you realize that even as you pray, God hears and answers your prayers? We conclude that His answer means no because the answer does not manifest in our timing; however, nothing could be further from the truth. God moves in His perfect timing. He already knew exactly what you needed even before you petitioned Him. Please understand, nothing surprises God. and there is nothing He does not already know about you and me.

My grandmother said to me many years ago, "If you ever want to know how much God knows all about you, read Psalm 139." Taking her advice, I attempted to read Psalm 139. It took me years of going back and forth trying to read the twenty-four verses. I would get stuck and cry. I would be in awe and overwhelmed. I would be ashamed and cry some more. I would be in amazement to see that the words would come off the pages of my Bible and become personal.

Psalm 139 gives a clear and vivid illustration of how detailed God knows each of us. The Holy Scriptures tell us, "We are searched and known, our thoughts are known from afar, He is acquainted with all our ways, wherever we are God is also, we have been made with fear and with wonder, our days have already been written and His thoughts toward us are more than the number of sands of the Earth."

That is how extremely intimate God knows you and me. I would say God deserves a wow. We just cannot get away from Him. He's everywhere we will be before we even get there. Knowing He is so close to me, reassures me that the process I am going through to reach my permanent promise is temporary. What God has for me is and was already planned by Him even while I was yet being formed in my mother's womb. That is how strategic He is in the details of our lives.

So, my question to you is, "What are you doing until the manifestation of your already answered prayer?"

I hear you asking, "What do you mean by already answered?"

The Bible tells us, "It shall come to pass that before they call, I will answer; and while they are still speaking, I will hear" (Isaiah 65:24). So, yes absolutely, your prayers are already answered.

I remember praying one morning during the WWPM 5am prayer. God said, "Lead them to pray bold prayers." So that is what I did, I led them to pray bold prayers.

Then God said, "And you pray bold prayers too."

To my surprise, I had not been praying as boldly as I thought. Praying what I thought were bold prayers, I would hear God say, "I have already answered that, pray bold prayers!"

I began to pray something else, and again, God would say, "I have already answered that too, PRAY BOLD PRAYERS!"

With God's seriousness and insistence for me to pray bold prayers, it got me thinking, "What am I not praying boldly for?" In the middle of praying for and leading others to pray bold prayers, the Holy Spirit dropped a truth in my spirit. "You have not prayed about your finances."

Wow, no, I had not. I had prayed for everyone else's finances, but I had failed to pray about my own. I immediately began praying earnestly for an area of my life I had overlooked many times, and just like that, I could feel the weight lift from me concerning what I had failed to pray for. As an intercessor, it can be easy to set your concerns aside while standing in the gap for others. So, I will ask you again, "What are you doing until the manifestation of the already-answered prayer?"

With that revelation, I considered how often I had heard folks give me excuses.

"I only pray when something is wrong."

"I only pray when there is a problem I cannot handle."

"I only pray when my life is completely out of my control."

I finally had to declare, "God is not your genie

in a bottle!"

Unfortunately, there are three areas of error people fall into in regard to prayer:

> 1) Some people do not pray at all.
>
> 2) Some people only pray when devastation happens.
>
> 3) Some people pray, but they do not believe God for the provision or the answer. In other words, they do not really believe God will (or can) come through for them.

What exactly does that say of our faith in our Heavenly Father? What exactly does that say of our belief in His uncompromising word? If we believe what Holy Scriptures tell us in 2 Corinthians 1:20 that "all the promises of God in Him are Yes, and in Him Amen, to the glory of God through us," then having a consistent praying life will establish a more intimate relationship with God. That closeness with God will strengthen your until something happens. Then receiving the manifestation of what you prayed for will further deepen your belief that His promises are certain.

His promises of certainty come with instructions. The Apostle Paul tells the church to pray without ceasing. Most hang on to those two words while still operating as if it is impossible to conceptualize what it means to pray without stopping or to always pray. Paul gave instructions to the church body to do several things while waiting for the coming of our Lord Jesus Christ. He charged us to "warn, uphold, be patient, do not retaliate, pursue what is good, rejoice, pray, and give thanks" (1 Thessalonians 5:14-18).

To pray without ceasing is to develop a consistent posture of prayer. Does it mean you are praying 24 hours daily, seven days a week? No! No one can do that and be part of a functioning society. You can, however, walk and live in a spiritual posture of prayer 24 hours a day. Having a posture of prayer is to have a spiritual state of mind of pressing into the presence of God. Being in this state will cause you to develop a deep desire to pray any and everywhere possible. You will not give a second thought about praying once you have been in the presence of God consistently. You will find yourself available to talk to and hear from God as you go throughout your day.

As I begin my day of devotion at 4:00am, while the house and many of those I intercede for are still asleep, I seek God diligently. Hebrews 11:6 reminds me to diligently seek Him because He is a Rewarder. I was once told by a dear sister-friend Gerri, "Your prayer life is abnormal."

I thought, *How offensive! Abnormal prayer life? How could that be?*

She explained. "Before I met you, I thought my prayer life was good. That was of course until we met. You really do pray without ceasing, and that is not normal. What I do is normal, what you do is abnormal."

Realizing her odd clarification, I received the compliment with my chest stuck out proudly. What would you expect or think if someone told you that you had an abnormal prayer life? You may think immediately, *Am I praying wrong, or what am I doing that is so abnormal?*

Those who are called to the ministry of intercessory prayer will certainly have an abnormal prayer life. Nothing about the intercessor's life is normal. The phone is constantly ringing, and the inbox is overflowing. People will recognize you in public places and ask you to pray for them. God wakes you in the middle of a good and restful sleep alerting you to trouble. What is the intercessor's response? We get up and pray.

Abnormal may seem like a strange word regarding prayer. Too often I have been asked to pray for someone simply because they knew their lifestyle would have to change. Prayer requires a lifestyle of holiness, which can be hard or even uncomfortable for some. Holiness says, "I am putting God before all else." The intercessor is telling the devil, "To get to them, you have to come through me first." That, my friend, is the blessed calling and banner of the intercessor. Those who dedicate themselves to constant devotion unto God through prayer will find life much easier to handle even in the difficult times.

Intercessors are given the honor of being watchmen on the wall keeping an eye over the city, region, or territory. Every time intercessors pray, they upset the kingdom of Hell. This is the job of the intercessor, we upset Hell. While it may not be glamorous, it is rewarding. Intercessors pray boldly and without ceasing. Others receive the blessing for which the intercessor has prayed, while the intercessor receives a favored trust from God that says He has certainly prepared the pray-er for such a task.

I do not take this calling lightly, haphazardly, or without regard. As an intercessor, I am being led by the Holy Spirit to cause a shift in the atmosphere in someone else's life. That type of spiritual discipline can be too weighty for some. I am a prayer warrior. I am a prophetic intercessor. I am a praying prophet. I am an atmosphere shifter. I am who God called me to be long before I was born.

Do you know who you are? Do you know what God has called you to? Do you know how powerful you are for the Kingdom of God? Get acquainted with God and yourself until *YOUR* something happens. There is a legacy within you to shift the trajectory of what you see now and what is to come. No more sitting back; get up and shift the atmosphere! Whether you are a stealth or a fighter jet, God has and is preparing you for greatness. Get ready for His level of excitement.

DAWN L. CRUMBLE

Chapter 3
Pray - The Ultimate Conversation

Welcome to a life of praying—a life that is consistent, strategic, and devoted to praying to be exact. I will often refer to having or living a praying lifestyle. What is the difference between prayer and praying? Prayer is the occupation. Praying is what we do in the occupation. And since prayer is an occupation that does not go away, we must have a praying lifestyle. Before I understood what prayer was, I wanted and expected my prayers to be answered quickly and in the exact way I wanted them answered. Consider the fact that praying is our responsibility and our charge to meet with God. He wants to spend intimate, quality time with us. Here are my three keys to a thriving praying life.

Relationship with God

A successful, fulfilling praying life is having a relationship with God. Praying is our direct line of communication with God. The occupation of prayer requires a relationship and having a relationship with anyone requires communication. Without communication, there is no relationship and without a relationship, there is no occupation.

Think of your prayer as your occupation and you have three significant others in your business: God is your CEO, Jesus is your manager, and the Holy Spirit is your co-laborer. To function effectively and efficiently in your position, you must have a daily briefing with your CEO, manager, and co-laborer. In these briefings, you discuss everything imaginable, from what is current to what is coming down the pipeline. The more and more you meet with your CEO, manager, and co-laborer, the more solidified and personal your relationship becomes. In this relationship, your life will be more fulfilled, more challenged, and more stable. To be fulfilled, challenged, and stable you cannot do life without this relationship built on communication, nor should you want to.

Faith in God

A successful, fulfilling praying life is having faith in God. Throughout the Bible, you will find numerous scriptures on faith. My personal favorite is Hebrews 11:6. "But without faith it is impossible to please Him, for he who comes to God must believe that He is, and that He is a rewarder of those who diligently seek Him." This scripture makes it clear that without faith it is impossible to please God.

When we do not apply or activate our faith in God, we are saying, "God, we do not trust you to handle what we're asking of You. We have more faith in man than in God. In fact, we never thought You would come through for us anyway." Those statements are doubt-filled and will ultimately contradict our prayers. If we allow our thoughts, people, and circumstances to contradict our prayers, why pray? We invite reckless doubt into our atmosphere the moment we determine God is not and cannot answer our prayers.

To this I say, if you are going to pray earnestly and sincerely, do not doubt God's power, God's timing, or God's promises. To have this type of "throw caution to the wind" faith, you must have a faith-filled praying life. Hebrews 11:6 finishes by saying "He is a rewarder of those who diligently seek Him." As you seek God diligently, expect your reward.

Consistent

A successful, fulfilling praying life is consistency. In *Draw the Circle: The 40 Day Prayer Challenge*," author Mark Batterson says, "If you pray to God regularly, irregular things will happen on a regular basis." Can you imagine getting your prayers answered just because you pray to God regularly? The consistent key is important as it relates to your praying life and your relationship with God. Do you have friends who only come to you when they need you to assist them, provide for them, or make something happen for them? If they are only coming to you when they are in need, you may be reluctant to help them with their requests. How would you feel if God said to you, "Since you only talk to me a little, I will only bless you a little?"

We may ask what is the point of praying anyway if God will not bless me the way I want? Consistent prayer is not about getting what we want, but rather it's about developing a relationship with God as our Heavenly Father. In Psalm 34:4, David sought the Lord; God heard David and delivered him from all his fears. David's pursuit of God was relentless, not because he wanted something from God, but because he desired a closer relationship with God. Seeking God consistently through prayer develops that relationship. If you do not have dedicated time for devotion and prayer, set an alarm and be intentional about making a regular, consistent appointment with Him. As you pursue God, He will pursue you.

Pray Until Something Happens

Now that I have shared my keys with you, let's get started on praying until something happens. The prayer need has presented itself, and we have answered the call to pray. Now the waiting begins. However, we are not waiting for the answer because God has already answered. We may not know the answer for certain, but God has answered. Jesus tells us, "For your Father knows the things you have need of before you ask Him" (Matthew 6:8).

Because God knows our needs even before we ask about them, once we do ask, we must trust Him and wait. Waiting can be a hard realization of God's perfect timing. In the middle of God's perfect timing (not permissive timing) is the absolute best place you can be. Pray, believe, trust, and have faith in God because our prayer is already answered. "Though it tarries, wait for it," says the prophet in Habakkuk chapter two, verse 3. While the answer may seem to be taking its sweet time, when God promises a thing, it will surely come to pass, and the blessing cannot be reversed (Numbers 23:20). FYI—answered prayers do not mean stop praying, it means God is preparing you until He delivers on His promises. That is a definite and certain promise of God.

What is Prayer?

I was asked, and I will ask you the same, "Are you praying out of routine or with intention?" Every day, even with a set praying and devotion time, we must pray with absolute intention and expectation. With intentional praying, "let your request be made known to God," the Apostle Paul instructs us in Philippians 4:6. It is important to learn to pray with intention, strategy, and purpose. With these, every prayer you pray, you will shift Heaven and you will upset Hell.

That is exactly what happened with Paul and Silas in the Book of Acts in chapter sixteen. This is a relatable story for many. On their way to prayer, they encountered an uncomfortable situation with a young girl. A slave herself, this young girl recognized and followed Paul and Silas for days. This encounter would delay them in getting to their destination but would not deter them from their mission or dampen their spirits. Their destination was a prayer meeting, but their assignment was to intercede and share the Gospel of Jesus Christ. When the demonic spirit in the girl recognized them as servants of God, Paul and Silas stopped her by casting the demon out. The girl's owners got mad because their source of income was now gone, so they had Paul and Silas arrested.

Being locked up and shackled became their instant way of living, or at the very least, a way of existing. Considering this, all the other prisoners around them probably knew who they were, probably wondered where their God was now, and probably concluded their days were numbered as disciples of Christ.

Most people in Paul and Silas's situation would have been infuriated. But then, at midnight, their prayers and worship while in the prison caused a supernatural earthquake amid their bad situation, right there in their imprisonment, and their delay swung open the doors of their jailhouse, setting them free. During their imprisonment, however, they remained focused on the assignment and did not waiver. They continued their task even though they were facing great opposition. Paul and Silas were in a place of desperation but were not desperate. They were surrounded by onlookers possibly questioning how they would get out of their predicament.

Often, we can find ourselves in similar situations—imprisoned, bound, shackled, and facing ridicule, judgment, and backlash. All through our ordeals, God surrounds us with many looky-loos, some waiting to witness our victories, but many waiting to celebrate our failures. We can be like Paul and Silas, praying and singing while imprisoned with witnesses looking on. These witnesses get to participate in our deliverance, in our salvation, and in our rescue. With our deliverance and rescue, comes their deliverance and rescue. That is what God does, He delivers us from our situation and even delivers those around us who are watching. Wow, what a powerful God we serve! Endeavor to be like Paul and Silas, then watch how your prayers and worship will supernaturally cause an earthquake to shift Heaven in your direction!

That is what prayer does for us, prayer shifts Heaven in our direction—in our favor. Remember, there is an upset in Hell with every prayer we pray. That is what prayer does for us. Our prayers and our consistent praying lifestyle upsets Hell. The enemy of our souls would rather us not pray at all. That is neither the answer nor is it the solution to our problems. The answer is praying and praying with diligence, intent, strategy, clarity, and purpose. I will also stress to you, pray for results. The answer is having a consistent praying lifestyle. Whew, all of that while you hear from God and patiently wait.

Pray Without Ceasing

First Thessalonians 5:17 tells us to "pray without ceasing." Exactly what are we praying for and why can't we stop praying? Whatever we are praying for, we must do so with strategy, intent, and clarity. We cannot stop because stopping means we are giving up, we are settling, and we have concluded that God is not answering our prayers. As an intercessor, the Holy Spirit gives and leads us in prayer. He tells us what to pray, how long to pray, and when to stop. While you are trying to figure out what you are praying for, God is revealing, teaching, and allowing you to go through so you will be able to get to the other side of what you are praying for.

What is on the other side of your prayers?

Many will pray for healing; God has a solution

for healing.

Many will pray for deliverance; God has a solution for deliverance.

Many will pray for finances; God has a solution for finances.

Many will pray for their children; God has a solution for your (or should we say His) children.

Many will pray for what they see as impossible; God has a solution for our impossible situations.

God's solutions are in His word. Through consistent prayer and His word, we will experience His solutions for our healing, deliverance, money issues, children, and so much more.

What is on the other side of your prayers? How wide is the valley you must cross before reaching the other side of your prayers? How deep is the ocean you must cross before reaching the other side of your prayers? The width and depth may be one of the hardest spiritual prayer paths you will cross, but you will cross, and you will get to the other side of your ocean and valley with heavenly victory.

Think of the crossing over as actually going through. Just like in Isaiah 43:2, "When you pass through...when you walk through..., fear not, for I am with you." This is what I call God's promise of certainty. When God gives His reassurance of being with us, we can rest knowing that whatever we are facing, going through, experiencing, or being overwhelmed by, He is with us as we make it to the other side. The beauty in that passage of scripture is one word: "through."

Too often we hear someone say what they are going through. They are making a pronouncement over their life when they are facing an unbearable struggle, hard times, loss, death, and barrenness. What they fail to realize is that going through is the beginning of God's solution. Since it is a known fact that they are going through, their continued walking through says there is a destination. God does not allow us to go through by leaving us in one place with no destination in sight.

God has a plan, and you are included in His plan. Keep praying while you are going through. Before you know it, you will have gone through, and you will find yourself on the shore of the other side of your going through. You will have arrived at your God-given destination.

As a little girl growing up on the spiritual foundation of my grandparents, I learned to kneel and pray. I learned to read my Bible. I learned the gospel hymns. One day I heard my grandmother say with Holy Spirit-filled confidence, "Let me pray about it and hear what God has to say." I knew, even as a little girl at the young age of seven, that that is what I wanted. I desired that power and authority to say, "Let me pray about it," and people would listen and be okay with that proclamation. Hearing my grandmother make that one statement solidified my desire and passion for prayer. At that young age, I knew there was something about this thing called prayer and that "something" was powerful. I wanted to know how to pray and how prayer worked, who I would pray to, and what would happen when I prayed. Prayer became my passion and my calling even at seven years old.

Prayer Mantle

It was not until many years later when my grandmother asked me, "Baby, are you still praying?" I answered yes but did not understand the reasoning behind her question. Little did I realize my grandmother's prayer mantle would become twins' fathertle to cover the five generations of our family.

Mantles are symbolic of a spiritual gift and mantles can be passed to another. Mantles are heavy and can be overwhelming to your physical body and your spirit man. Mantles can make or break you. What will it be for you? Mantles can leave a legacy for generations to come. Are you ready? Have you considered your mantle? What do they feel like and look like? To whom will you leave your prayer mantle? Are they ready for the mantle of prayer? Or is prayer like a foreign language and looked at only as a casual pastime? Let's change that today.

Ask God to explain to you your prayer mantle. Also ask Him who you need to prepare to accept your mantle. Your prayer mantle gives you supernatural boldness, power, position, authority, protection, and respect.

To understand this mantle, take a look at Elijah and Elisha. Elisha stayed close to his mentor Elijah. Elisha watched and learned from the miracles he performed, listened to his prayers, and witnessed his relationship with God. Elisha reached further and desired to carry a double portion of Elijah's spirit (or anointing) after Elijah's death took him to be with God. This is the way your mantle (or glory) will rest on who's next to carry yours.

When we think of mantles, we can think they

may be "too much to bear," when in all actuality, our mantle is written into our spiritual DNA. While we may feel inadequate to carry the mantle or glory of prayer, we are designed, established, and ordained by God for such a time as this. And then we are to pass our mantle on at the appointed time to the appointed carrier.

Prayer appointments, calling, and assignments ordained by God are not something from which you can run. Trust me, I tried, and over the course of many years, God still reminded me one Saturday morning when I asked, "Lord, what do you want me to do?" I heard the Lord say with absolute clarity, "What you are supposed to be doing." Somehow, I was hoping God had changed His mind, but I was not surprised when the answer was the same as what I had said yes to in 1989. That year was very transformational, filled with loss, healing, deliverance, hurt, betrayal, and repentance. All of that and the years to follow resulted in a lifestyle of devoted prayer.

> *"Just as we would not assume someone could live a holy life without prayer, how can someone pray but not live a holy life?" ~William Law, A Serious Call to a Devout and Holy Life*

DAWN L. CRUMBLE

Chapter 4
Prophesy - Speak Life

Some look at the word "prophesy" as spooky, something only certain people can use, or something a few people are blessed to have as a spiritual gift from God. I was in my early twenties the first time God gave me a prophetic word for someone. I did not see it as a prophetic word or as prophesy, because I did not see myself as a prophet. One thing I did know was the voice of God. That night sitting in revival, I heard clear instructions from God. I rushed home to share with my mother the urgency of my delivering the word. The next day we drove four hours to make sure the word was delivered. And with that one act of obedience, the river of spiritual gifts began to flow. Little did I realize I spoke life into someone's valley of dry bones. That experience gave them insight into the plans God had for their life.

My grandmother Allie would say, "Not one thing is too hard for God." Let me encourage you by saying there is absolutely nothing too hard for God. The story of Ezekiel and the valley of dry bones (chapter 37) is so familiar to some that key points to this victory can be overlooked. Ezekiel was a prophet and priest at the worst time in Judah's history. God uses Ezekiel to deliver His word to His people who have gone astray to reconcile them back to Himself. While in the worst position imaginable, God knew His people had potential and gave instructions on how to revive a dry and dead army.

When we think there is no hope, all of a sudden, we hear the rumbling in the winds and our hard places become alive once again, just like the army of Israel. If God can instruct Ezekiel to speak life into a valley of a dead army, He can and will instruct you also to breathe life back into your valley of a dead situation. And since this is true, why can't we believe God for supernatural power and deliverance in our hard places? We can, we just need some help.

Put yourself in Ezekiel's place. In fourteen verses God came upon him, brought him out in the Spirit of the Lord, set him down in the midst of the valley, and caused him to pass by them all. We may immediately ask why God did all of that in the first two verses. Sometimes God has to move us quickly to get our attention to His detail in the stuff we face. If God moves too slowly for us, we forget and lose focus. In Ezekiel's case, God had to move quickly because there was work Ezekiel had to do, not only for himself but for the valley he was in. God gives us clear instructions on what, when, where, who, why, and how to handle every situation we are facing.

Just as God set Ezekiel down in the middle of

his difficult time, so He does with us. Anytime God is preparing you for a miracle, He will certainly have His hand upon you. Anytime you are going into battle, He will most definitely have His hand upon you. What battle you ask? It could be your home, work, children, health, or finances. You name it, and there is the potential for a battle. There will be times in which you will feel you are in this thing alone. It will be overwhelming, it will be painful, it will appear bigger than it is, and it will be hard. Be encouraged, child of God. With God's hand on your life and in your situation, you are assured that you are not in your valley alone. If God be for you, who can be against you (Romans 8:28)? It gives an assurance that since His promises are yes (2 Corinthians 1:20), all you have to do is agree with an amen to His promises for your future. It gives an assurance that He is not a man that He should lie… (Numbers 23:19). It gives an assurance that you in fact can do all things through Christ…(Philippians 4:13). When you know the hand of God is upon you it gives an assurance to carry on! Since God's promises are yes, all you have to do is agree with an amen to His promises for your future. He is not a man that He should lie. God's hand on your life gives an assurance that you, in fact, can do all things through Christ. You have assurance to carry on when you know the hand of God is upon you.

    God will give clear instructions to prophesy to every situation we are facing in our valley. How do we do this? I am so glad you asked. It is time our spiritual bones hear the word of the Lord. That is exactly how God told Ezekiel to prophesy, "O dry bones, hear the word of the Lord!"

We get through our valleys, disappointments, and challenges, through earnest and diligent prayer. The best prayer prayed is the word of the Lord, right out of the Holy Scriptures. Hard as it may be, seem, or feel, prayer still and always works in our favor. And the best way to experience complete healing, deliverance, restoration, and so much more is to give your situation the word of God. Isaiah 55:11 says, "So shall My word be that goes forth from My mouth; it shall not return to Me void, but it shall accomplish what I please, and it shall prosper in the thing for which I sent it." This is a promise of certainty, an invitation and promise to an abundant life.

Prophesy to your dry places. Prophesy to the dead places. Prophesy to the places that challenge you the most. Prophesy and watch God meet and exceed your expectations.

The valley experience is interesting. Just like with Ezekiel, God set him down in the middle of his valley—his hard place and his bad experience—and you too will find yourself in the middle of your valley of dry bones. The good thing is since God set you there, He is also there with you. In the most difficult places, it usually feels as though God has forgotten about you, but the scriptures say, "He will never leave you, nor will He forsake you."

What expectations do you have of God? Do you have expectations of healing? Expectations of provision? Expectations to be saved and rescued? Expectations galore are upon us everywhere we go. In every situation, you should expect greater. Some would conclude, "Why expect anything from God? I am happy with whatever and however He blesses me." That is completely okay; however, consider this: since Ephesians 3:20 declares "Him who is able to do exceedingly abundantly above all we ask or think," why then should you be satisfied with the small things?

God wants us to pray big and pray boldly. God wants us to prophesy to the hard places in our lives. God wants more and has more for you and me. We can expect more than what we are asking for. It is time to prophesy to the difficult thing, and it is also time to encourage ourselves with the promises of God.

What would your life look like if you went from complacency and comfortability to expecting signs and wonders? That is precisely what prophesying does for us. It transitions us from one level of expectation to the next. It elevates us to believe in God for the greater. It propels, launches, and catapults us to a place where we will not and cannot be without the help of God. If we are not doing so already, we can start prophesying to our hard place today. The hard place is waiting for a supernatural release, a supernatural deliverance, a supernatural thrust.

Are you ready for what God has for you? Prophesy, child of God, to your hard place!

I had to learn to prophesy to my hard places and believe the word of God. Let me challenge you to dive into your Bibles for the answers to your hard places. That is where we will find situations, answers, resolve, encouragement, and promises.

God's word is a bright revelation and will shift atmospheres in your favor. When you believe the word of God, prophesying to your hard, difficult places becomes so much easier. And though you may still be in the process of the hard place, knowing that God has promised to be with you makes the process worth the journey. I have heard it said, "I am not where I want to be, but thank God, I am not where I used to be." God wants us to hold on to that sentiment. Hold on to God's promises which, by the way, are prophetic. Like King David, you will need to encourage yourself in God's word, and you will need to encourage others around you.

How do you encourage yourself through the prophetic? What makes it so special, so desired, so necessary? When we consider the gift of prophecy, the word says, "But he who prophesies speaks edification and exhortation and comfort to men" (1 Corinthians 14:3). Some find it hard to believe or receive a prophetic word, simply because they are in a rush for the manifestation. God is not a microwave god. He is, however, the God of suddenly, immediately, and now. His timing is not our timing. Wait on God! This is why it is important to understand your hard place and what you are desperate for. A place of desperation will push you to believe God for the impossible and hear His voice clearer. You will prophesy out of your desperation and out of that desperation, you will find yourself growing and glowing closer to God. Get in a deliberate habit of asking God to help you understand where you are and why you are there. As we come to understand the where and the why, we will begin to pray differently, with strategy and intent. We will begin to prophesy differently. We will begin to live, respond, and expect differently. We will hear God more clearly once we understand more clearly.

Have you ever received a prophetic word and wondered to yourself, "How did they know that?" Or, "When will this happen?" Or, "I do not see how that will even happen." Then all of a sudden, or maybe years later, you experience the manifestation of what God promised. God does it for you when you least expect it, but He always comes through on time. Never discount or throw away God's promises because they do not happen in your time. God's timing is perfect—never late and never early. The best place to be is in His perfect timing. His timing is everything. His promises will surely come to fruition; wait for them!

DAWN L. CRUMBLE

Chapter 5
Praise Is What We Do

One of my favorite passages of Scripture is Psalm 34, particularly verses one through four. Many of the verses explain perfectly the five W's and one H that defines praising the Lord.

1) I will bless the LORD at all times;
His praise *shall* continually *be* in my mouth.
2) My soul shall make its boast in the LORD;
The humble shall hear *of it* and be glad.
3) Oh, magnify the LORD with me,
And let us exalt His name together.
4) I sought the LORD, and He heard me,
And delivered me from all my fears.

Did you see the five W's and one H?

WHO is to praise the Lord? You, me, everybody.

WHAT does praise consist of? Bless and boast.

WHEN are we to praise the Lord? Continually.

WHERE are we to praise the Lord? With others.

WHY praise the Lord? He hears and delivers.

HOW are we to praise the Lord? With our mouths, and in our souls.

The opening verses of Psalm 34 set the tone about praise. "I will bless the Lord at all times." Think about that. To say "I will" means we are declaring what we are committing to. Psalm 34 is entitled "The Happiness of Those Who Trust in God."[1] It is our promise to God of our urgency to praise Him regardless of what is going on before, behind, or beside us. We declare that we will praise Him. To say "I will" means we have made a conscious decision to always bless the Lord. No matter what the times may look like, we shared our decision, and our decision is admirable.

Praisers reminisce on what God has done either for them or for someone close. This is what Psalm 34:4 is referring to when it says, "Oh, magnify the Lord with me, and let us exalt His name together." There is beauty in praising the Lord with and for someone else's blessing, their good health report, the salvation of a loved one, or the purchase of a new home. What David did was invite others to praise the Lord with him. Have you been in that position where you insisted upon wanting someone to praise the Lord with you for His goodness? Testimony after testimony of God's goodness and loving-kindness toward you will cause a praise breakout and develop

---

[1] *Hebrew-Greek Key Word Study Bible* NKJV, AMG, 2015.

your praise posture. That posture is vitally important to the success of *your* until-something-happens journey.

Seven Postures of Praise

Many of the praise scriptures are in the Psalms. Numerous times when David found himself in situations in which nobody but God could save him, he cried out, he pleaded, and he even danced. Psalm 34 shows many of the praise postures when David offers his confessional praise (Yada) in verse one and goes on to invite others into his praise party by bidding, "Oh, magnify the Lord with me." There are seven means by which we offer our praise to God.

1. Toda – praise of thanksgiving.
2. Yada – an outward and vigorous confession of praise with our hands lifted or extended to God: "I will," "I shall."
3. Barak – a quiet worshipful praise, blessing God bowed down before His presence.
4. Sabah – our battle cry praise in which our whole being is in our praise.
5. Zamar – praise that makes the instruments sing.
6. Halal – our boastful, soul praise until we look foolish.
7. T'hilla – when God takes residence in our praise, proclaiming His excellence.

I remember dreaming of owning my own home, which, by the way, I had concluded would only come via marriage. Purchasing on my own was never a thought because I bought every bad resolution as to

why it would not happen:
- I did not have the income.
- My credit was horrible.
- I am a single black woman.

On and on I went, setting up my own roadblocks to homeownership. I guess I thought I did not have what it took to be a homeowner. But God's timing was my immediate lesson and my reassurance to remember God's promises.

Months before applying for a home loan, Pastor Swanigan prophesied, "God is going to erase the bad credit, clear up debt, and make all things new."

My pastor's prophesy was a good word, and while I received it, I did not ponder on it. But when I checked my credit report (all three of them), I was expecting the same bad, horrible, and low credit score. To my utter shocking surprise, over $27,000 in debt had been erased as if it was never there. Poof! It was gone. I looked for it and examined my credit reports. It was completely gone, wiped out. What happened I do not know and did not have a clue. Then my daughter Sydney reminded me of the prophetic word, "Mommy, remember what the pastor said?"

God Surprises

Immediately, rejoicing overwhelmed me, and my spirit began singing praises to the Lord. Tears were streaming and yes, I was doing the ugly cry. Sydney and I applied for the home loan together. And while I was hopeful, I still needed to hear the mortgage lender say the words, "You are approved. Now go shopping." Those were the most exciting simple sentences I'd ever heard.

God's surprises are so real. And that is not the end. I tried preparing myself for a bidding war in the very competitive California housing market. We made an offer of $5,000 over the asking price.

Surprise number two from God—there were no other offers, and ours was immediately accepted.

Surprise number three—the appraisal returned less than the asking price, opening the door for the original price to decrease.

Surprise number four—the inspection came back with a few minor hazardous repairs and the owner made all the repairs.

Surprise number five—the owner gave $5,000 toward the closing costs.

All this happened in less than thirty days. And just days before leaving for London, England, to minister, we closed. I had never signed my name so many times. The tears streamed, and my spirit lept again. I would finally be a homeowner. While sitting at San Francisco International Airport, our real estate agent called and announced, "I have your keys." Halal praise erupted in the Virgin Atlantic terminal.

One surprise after another built my praise posture. Even now, as I walk through my home, my soul makes its boast in the Lord daily. God did it His way and in His timing. And guess what? I have always wanted to live in a cul-de-sac in a gated community. Yep, again God said, "Surprise!"

Sometimes the tables in your life will turn all the way upside down, leaving you with fear, doubt, frustration, and insecurity. These are demonic strongholds that can take up residence in your life if you allow them. However, praising God in the most awful times will propel you into a closer relationship with Him, shift atmospheres, and cause others to wonder about your God. The older saints would say, "God is a wonder in my soul." Yes, He is. I can attest to that. My lips shall praise You.

When thinking of what must be done until the manifestation of your already-answered prayer, praising the Lord comes to mind. In Psalm 63, David explains his joy in fellowship with God. To fellowship in the presence of God, there must be a relationship with God. And when there is a relationship with God, you are able to better understand who God is and how He loves you.

Praise is what you must do. Can you imagine and reflect on what has or will cause you to praise God when everything around you has fallen apart? With falling apart going on around you, you can easily forget or neglect to praise your way through to your victories. Life can certainly be overwhelming and that is expected, but what you offer God in place of your overwhelmed feelings will thrust you into your eternal victory. The answer for uncomfortable circumstances is to praise your way through. Praising until *your* something happens will cause a catapult effect that will forever transform your life. It is time to get your praise on!

Why do you praise the Lord? Because praise is what you were created to do. Praising in humble, reverent submission will take you into the realm of God's presence where miracles happen. Praise God during various times in your life and in the most honoring ways. The beauty in praising God is to reverence God for who He is and what He has done in your life. The hardest times to offer your praise to God are when you are faced with difficult situations. Life's circumstances, the world's view, doubters, what you see in the natural, and of course, the devil will always try to convince you that you are better off succumbing to failure, loss, defeat, and everything else that has been shoved into your existence. When all this is happening, you absolutely must declare, "I will bless the Lord at all times!"

People somehow believe they know what is best for you, your problems, your struggles, and your hardships. Looking in from the outside, others will find it unusual for you to be in a place of madness, chaos, and confusion, all while praising God through it. So, what does praise look like when you are in your moment of depression, agony, and pain? You have been hurt, disappointed, and devastated. What does praise look like now when you would rather throw your hands up and scream "I give up!?"

I urge you, do not throw in the towel, and do not give up. Praise honors God for who He is, what He has done, what He is doing, and what He is yet to do in your life. At the same time, your praise will cause your enemies—foreign, domestic, natural, and supernatural—to flee in confusion. Just think about David dancing before the Lord and Jehoshaphat sending the praisers to set an ambush around their enemies before going into battle.

Just as much as you should live in a posture of praise, praise is also your weapon. Use it daily. It is powerful! Praise the Lord when everything is going extremely well and praise the Lord in your saddest moment. Whatever you do, praising the Lord works in your favor.

Overcomers praise when others relax in the face of defeat. Victors praise when victims wallow in despair. Winners win while wimps bow out gracefully. Repeat after me:

I am an overcomer. God made me an overcomer. I am a victor. God made me victorious. I am a winner. God made me a winner and winners always win. I am a praiser. God created me to praise Him and that I will do daily. Amen!

Chapter 6
Press Into His Presence

On April 21, 2015, God spoke to me about "the press." In my prayer time, I got a clearer understanding of what it means to press into God's presence. These are the instructions the sovereign God told me:

"Press into my presence, there I will do great things for you.
Press into my presence, there I will do marvelous things for you.
Press into my presence, there is where I heal.
Press into my presence, there I will release blessings beyond your resources.
Press into my presence, there I will release my favor.
Press into my presence, there I will give you the desires of your heart.
Press into my presence, I will use you for my

glory.

Press into my presence, there I will change your anointing.

Press your way into my presence each day."

With all that pressing into God's presence, an overflow of His blessings is on the horizon for you and me. Let us press into God's presence together.

Press is both a noun and a verb. As a noun, we see the press as a device for applying pressure. Just like with olives, to get the finest quality of olive oil, the presser selects the best olives at their ripest, presses them, then separates them from the oil and water. This is contrary to the type of press that God takes us through when He selects us. He selects us in our immaturity (pre-ripeness), presses us (going through trials), and then separates us from what is of no good for us. And just like the olive, there are levels of the pressing process for us. In the *first press* there is crushing, but only once; we call this salvation.

As a verb, we see the press as a cause to move into a position of contact with something by exerting continuous physical force. What does it mean for the child of God to get into a pressing position? It means even in the hardest of times, God will extract His best from us to get us to our destiny. It means we are not only pressed for ourselves but for those in the press with us and those coming behind.

Then, there is the cold press. This is the press that never exceeds 80° Fahrenheit. We can easily see our lives as a crushed olive from which God extracts all that is good. The crush does not kill us, instead it makes us better for everyone who will experience the goodness of the Lord through us. The cold-pressed olives are also crushed but since they do not experience as much heat, they retain more of their nutrients. This is the child of God who is least resistant to God's teachings, does not require the heated press, and is more flavorful and potent.

There is something very special about pressing into the presence of the living God. Are you ready for the press? Are you ready to get into position before God?

When writing the dedication page for the *Women Who Pray* journal, I talked about pressing into the presence of God. Well, the editor—who was a sweet lady who had never experienced the press—decided to change the word "press" to the word "lean." I quickly called her to make her change it back. She responded, "Press is not grammatically correct. Lean is easier to read."

The spirit of correction came upon me. "Girl, this is not about being grammatically correct. We do not *lean* into God's presence, we press!"

I guess she heard something in my voice that convinced her that our dealings with God is not just a casual, off-hand "lean." I could sense her mind and heart telling her, *I had better change the word before she comes through the phone.* She did. It was at that moment I had to give a quick lesson on pressing into the presence of God and that lesson remains even in my spirit.

One thing I know for sure is there is nothing like the press. You must want to be in it, be desperate for it, and expect something powerfully life-changing while in it. You must want bigger, exceedingly abundantly above what you ask or think. The press is a transformational place. It is the place of intimate communion with God where you will experience the complete deliverance, healing, and restoration of the living God. It is the place where you will encounter His glory.

The press can be uncomfortable, but there is a reward on the other side of the press. You must be determined to get into the press. You must have what I call "desperate determination." Being desperate for the presence of God will get you to one place, but when you couple it with determination, you will care nothing about what people think or say about you, and care more about what God says and thinks about you.

We are familiar with the woman with the issue of blood. The Bible tells us that this woman was afflicted with an issue of flowing blood for twelve years. Now, suffering from something for twelve years for the 21st century woman is unheard of and certainly unbearable. This woman had spent all her hard-earned money on doctors without any resolution. As the story goes on, Jesus was coming her way, headed to heal someone else. I am guessing this woman did not care what the townspeople would say, what they would do, or what they would think. She gained enough strength to get into the press of people that surrounded Jesus. This woman was sick and tired of being sick and tired, and she pressed and crawled her way into the presence of the Savior, Jesus Christ.

Not only was this woman desperate, but she also

was determined. She was desperate enough to forget about her surroundings, and she was determined enough to crawl to the One she knew to be a healer. On her knees and engulfed by the multitudes of people, she pressed her way to Jesus. She knew she had one shot at getting His attention. She knew within herself, *If I could just grab onto the hem of His garment, I will be healed.*

With His hem in her sight, this woman who had suffered all that time reached out and grabbed what she knew to be her answer. As the healing virtue of Jesus left His body, she got His attention and immediately her affliction stopped.

Can you imagine, after twelve long years of trying everything you thought would work, spending your entire savings, and going to every doctor far and near, just one touch of the Savior's robe immediately ending your years-long battle? That is exactly what pressing into the presence of God will get us: the attention of Jesus and an immediate experience. The ultimate resolve must be that you are completely desperate and determined beyond your circumstances to get in the press. Do you have that desperate determination or are you just sitting around, hoping one day Jesus will pass you on the road?

Not sure yet? Let's look at another account. The previous woman we just investigated had a physical malady. This next man was possessed by so many demons, the demons called themselves Legion.

This young man lived in a cave, although some say more accurately, he lived in the tombs or the graveyard. Whether his home was a cave, a tomb, or a graveyard, anyway you slice it, his living situation was a dark place that was uncomfortable, dreary, scary, unattractive, and smelled of death. The townspeople placed him in shackles trying to restrain him.

Have you ever been in a situation where people tried to restrain you or keep you from your destination? This young man was another who had desperate determination in his spirit. Again, he did not care what people would say, do, or think. He was determined enough to be set free from the demons that possessed his body and mind. He was determined to meet Jesus.

Leaving the dark place of the tombs and knowing Jesus's boat would soon dock near Galilee, he pressed his way to the shore. Not caring about the onlookers, the squawkers, or those who preferred to keep him in chains, he pressed with desperate determination. The Bible says "he met Jesus."

Do you have that desperate determination to leave your dark place to meet Jesus or are you hoping one day Jesus will come into your tomb and graveyard to rescue you? Get in the press. Forget the naysayers around you and go meet Jesus. He is waiting for you. Being desperate for the presence of God will get you to one place, but desperate determination will get you an encounter with God. Come out of your dark place and get to where Jesus is. He is waiting for you.

In the press there is also something for us to achieve. The apostle Paul tells us to "press toward the goal for the prize of the upward call of God in Christ Jesus" (Philippians 3:14 NKJV). What prize, what goal, and what upward call? They all sound great, but pressing into the presence of God takes you one level at a time with the ultimate level being citizenship in Heaven.

The mark is your bullseye of precision that determines your destination. God sets the bullseye, and we are to work diligently at hitting the target on the designated assignment. Sometimes the assignments are short distances, while others are longer distances. Sometimes your mark is on a pendulum, always moving. You never know at the beginning which will be easier, and that is not the determining factor of the success of your hitting the target. The determining factor in your success is if you quit the assignment.

Just recently, I tried moving ahead of God because of my frustration. The outcome I wanted did not happen my way. While I believed I was ready for the promotion, God quickly reminded me, "You have not learned everything I need you to learn in this assignment. Where I am taking you, I need you to stay the course and learn everything in this position so you will be successful where I am taking you." It was a brief conversation, but necessary. My jumping ship and aborting the assignment was not an option. There was greater ahead of me, and the lives I would impact required me to stay in my current "ship."

Assignments from God are not meant to be abandoned when you find yourself in the press. Those assignments are meant to be completed unto the glory of the Lord. Each assignment comes with levels of completion, and the higher or harder the level, the tougher or bigger the assignment. That is exactly why many lose heart and jump ship before the assignment is complete. They have grown weary of the assignment, it is not happening the way they thought, or everyone around them is against what they are doing. Before they realize it, the white flag has been thrown and the assignment has been aborted.

Do not abort your assignment! You have a God-ordained assignment, and as much as you would like to get away from it, it is not going anywhere until you complete it. It is important that you remain in the press of your assignment because the bullseye is waiting for you.

Speaking of the bullseye, have you wondered who or what is on your bullseye? The goal may be for your spiritual growth, but the ultimate goal is most likely for someone else's salvation, healing, or deliverance. Our assignments are never solely about us. People are depending on us to finish our assignments and hit our targets. The more and more we hit the bullseye, the more and more we become a maximum impact for the Kingdom of God. Keep pressing toward the mark, the best prize is waiting at the finish line.

What is in the press for you? A glorious encounter with your Heavenly Father, an encounter that will surpass your understanding, and the understanding of those around us. In this press, there is fullness of joy and even when it seems like you should be falling apart and completely discombobulated, there is a joy in the press that cannot be explained. Others will wonder and ask, "This would have devastated me, why aren't you falling apart?" You will be experiencing God upholding you in trying times, times of despair, and times of frustration.

As you press your way into desperate determination for the presence of the Almighty God, you will find exactly what you need to get through to the place of peace, love, hope, and encouragement. Maybe you fail to get into the press because you feel you are undeserving. This is the farthest thing from the truth. You are deserving of God's love, His peace, and His hope. Mostly you deserve to be in God's presence because this is where you will encounter Him like never before.

Enjoy the press. It can be hard, but it is worth it. There are miracles, healing, laughter, and peace waiting for you in the press. Press in and watch what God will do in and through and by and for and with you. God promises you, "Eye has not seen, nor ear heard, nor have entered into the heart of man the things which God has prepared for those who love Him" (1 Corinthians 2:9).

Chapter 7
Process The Go Through

Whenever you are facing any sort of change, there is a process. Whether it is an address change, a job change, a relationship status change, the number of dependents change, a health change, or a financial change (increase or decrease), there is a process that is required to adjust. There is a process until something happens. And usually with change, there is discomfort; however, the one thing I know for sure, the process is temporary. For most, the process is uncomfortable, unbearable, unwanted, and unreasonable because it comes from the necessity and complacency of being in control.

Instinctively whenever, whatever, wherever, whyever and however changes occur, anxiety creeps in and rears its ugly head. Even if the change is for your good, anxiety somehow finds a crack in your sanity to cause dis-ease. A crack. In some cases, there may be multiple cracks or one huge sinkhole.

Regardless of the size or the quantity of the cracks, God is right there with you through the process, and the process is for you to get to the other side of what you are expecting God to do in your life. There is a destination to every process. And the other side of the process can be so close that we can see it and yet be so far away that we feel like it is unreachable. Why must we go through the process? What is the purpose of the process? And when is the process over?

Through: to continue in time toward the completion of a process. At times you may have said or heard others say, "I am *really* going through." To give a simple clarification, there is a struggle going on currently. No one likes the feeling of going through. Let me encourage you when you are going through whatever it may be, look on the brighter side. There is beauty in going through the process. According to Isaiah 43:2, "When you pass through the waters, I will be with you; and through the rivers, they shall not overflow you. When you walk through the fire, you shall not be burned, nor shall the flame scorch you." The word *when* confirms you will go through. The question is not if, but when. Again, there is beauty in going through. God is there with us. That's His promise of certainty. He will not leave, nor will He forsake us, but He will see that we get to the other side of our process. We must go through to stretch our faith, believe in God for the impossible, and prepare ourselves for the blessing.

If you do not go through it, you will not complete the process, and you will be stuck treading in the middle of the assignment and not getting anywhere. In Ephesians 3:20, the Bible tells us God is able to do "exceedingly abundantly above all we ask or think." Now if we are asking and thinking according to our vision and understanding, we will never get the exceedingly abundantly above all. Sadly, we will readily settle for what we see and understand. But this scripture tells us whatever we ask or think, God is able to do exceedingly abundantly more, so why not pray big? Why not pray bold? Why not pray with expectancy? The way I see it, God will always outdo what we see or understand. And that, my friend, is all part of the process. God must process you or take you through the process before the big blessing, the big breakthrough, the big promotion, the big house, the big healing, and especially the big overflow. Praying big will not only take you to the process but will take you through the process.

There is so much to learn in the process. Remember the process is temporary. I remember like it was yesterday, saying yes to ministry. Oh, and by the way, the process continues with each elevation, with each physical or spiritual promotion, and with each level of glory to glory to glory. But for now, let me share my story—my testimony—of the redemption process (my testimony).

My process began when I made one of the worst decisions of my life. I was completely lost in a relationship that was headed for nowhere, and those whom I thought were for me, made every bad decision easier and easier. Unfortunately, these were faithful church-going people who enabled me to spiral out of my control, but all the while God was still very much in control. Certainly, I asked God to forgive me, and I was confident that He would, but it was not until I learned to forgive myself that I truly experienced the redemptive love of Jesus Christ. And once I did, the process began.

That is exactly what God can and will do for you too. He will allow you to go through because there is the other side of your going-through that you must reach. He will allow you to be hurt, disappointed, and let down, all because there is the other side of your hurt and failure that will restore you and bless others in God's outcome. He will allow you to wonder what in the hell is going on. All because there is the other side of your pain that must be healed. When all is said and done, your process will be one of your greatest testimonies ever.

There is a process for everyone until something happens. The potter's wheel is a process. The widow woman had a process for her sons and her jar of oil. Queen Esther had a process to save her people. Ruth certainly had her process until Boaz noticed her. Jonah had his process called disobedience and big fish. The woman at the well, the woman with the issue of blood, and Mary the mother of Jesus all had their season of process.

And let us not forget the men of the scriptures. Peter, John, and Paul all had seasons of processes. But it was just that, a season, not a lifetime. The prophet Habakkuk tells us "though it tarries, wait for it; because it will surely come." Your process to your other side will seem like, feel like, look like, and sound like it is taking forever. Wait for it, because in your season of waiting, it is God's vision you are waiting for, not yours. I have learned not to be in a rush for the plan of God, but to wait for it. When you get into your rush, you can get out of alignment with God and find yourself struggling to stay afloat. Wait for it; it will surely come.

In this process, until something happens, God is preparing you for the next phase of your life. God is the potter, and you are His clay. The story of the prophet Jeremiah receiving the Word of the Lord at the potter's house shows that you, too, are like the clay on the wheel. The interesting thing about clay is the best clay is found deep within the earth, but still with impurities that must be kneaded out, pounded out, and beat out before it is even placed on the wheel.

There are four steps to your creation as a clay vessel: the kneading, the wheel, the molding, and finally the firing. Each of these steps heightens your process of moving forward. The earth of your soul is found in the deep, dark recesses of life in the same way as the best clay comes from deep within the earth. Reaching deep can be likened to giving God your wholehearted yes and your complete surrender.

Some are so convinced God could never use them because of the guilt and shame of past sins, that they find it hard to believe they are special and usable for and by God. You have so-called-supporting cast members (family and friends) who will conclude, "Never, ever could or would God use you." You have pre-determined that you will always be on the sideline and only those with some form of status will be trusted by God for any assignment. That is the furthest ideal from the truth. God can and will use whomever He pleases.

You have said yes and now the process of kneading, pounding, beating, and firing will begin. This may sound violent, but remember God is there with you every step of the process way. The kneading, pounding, beating, and firing of the body, soul, and mind can be overwhelming. You will probably begin to wonder if the process journey is worth it, if there can be an easier way to get through this. You'll wonder what will happen if you do not make it to the other side of your process. Just when you feel you cannot face another day or moment of the kneading, pounding, beating, and firing of your spiritual clay, you'll find yourself near the end, but the process will not be quite finished.

At this point, you will find yourself on the potter's wheel. It will feel like your life is spinning completely out of control, but never forget that you are in the tender and protective hands of your loving potter, Father God. This is how I visualize God as the Potter. You are this impure lump that requires a whole lot of shaping and molding. Father God is controlling the speed of the wheel of your life with His foot. As much as it feels like we are swirling, He has the velocity of every situation under His control. Sometimes the velocity slows to calm you, and at other times the velocity picks up. (Picture losing your wig; the spin is that fast!) Still, Father God is in complete control of every situation, every circumstance, every trial you are in, and those to come.

As God is controlling the spinning wheel with His foot on the wheel pedal, He has His right hand on the inside of you, shaping you from the inside out. This is where Psalm 51 happens: the mercy of God, the washing of your soul, your broken heart, and the cleansing of your mind. At the same time, Father God is using His left hand to mold you into who He has called you to be. While His right hand is preparing you on the inside, and His left hand is shaping you on the outside, He is also fighting off contaminants that would be a constant irritant, stumbling block, or hindrance in your walk with Him. Yes, Father God is more than ambidextrous. Both of His hands are shaping you while He is still going to war for you.

When the task of the wheel is complete, you are a beautiful vessel ready for use, ready to be poured into, and ready to be used to pour into someone else. You are a beautiful vessel. People will stop to stare at your distinction, your shine, your posture, and your ability to give and receive.

Do not be afraid of the process—it is there for you.

Do not be afraid of the process—you must get to the other side.

Do not be afraid of the process—it is temporary, and someone is waiting for your impact.

And what an impact you will be. Do not leave. The process is much easier with God than without. Let's get through the process together. Let's get to the other side of your assignment.

DAWN L. CRUMBLE

Chapter 8
Prepare for The Blessing

How do you or should you prepare for what you have already prayed for even though it has not manifested itself yet? I remember many years ago, my cousin prayed for all new furniture for her home. She prayed earnestly, believing that God one day would answer with a truckload of new furniture. The immediate problem was that her entire house was already completely furnished. Every room was complete. There was no room for anything new or old. Where would she put a houseful of new furniture?

Still, she continued praying. She even went window shopping getting ideas to take before God. Finally, when she was quiet long enough between her prayers and her plans to hear His voice, God said to her, "Daughter, you cannot fill a house that is already full. Get rid of what is blocking my answer."

It was that simple—she needed to first get rid of

what was blocking the manifestation of God's answer. So, she set every piece of her unwanted furniture on the curb for the weekly garbage pickup. Soon, to her surprise, she found out many neighbors and strangers desperately needed the furniture she was holding onto. One person's trash is indeed another person's treasure. The next day, my cousin went shopping for everything that was on her list. And without hesitation, God opened the once-closed door to bring her prayer list to fruition.

Have you ever done that? Prayed, and prayed, and prayed, and wondered why it seemed as if God was not listening and certainly not answering? What was the delay in getting what you were asking God for? What was happening in your life and in your circumstances that made God hold back His blessing? To be honest, God was not holding back His blessing or denying you. He was preparing you for greater.

It is easy to fall into the trap of only focusing on what you want and what you can wrap your mind around. Those thoughts are almost always much smaller than what God has for you. Since what God has for you is greater, there must be a preparation period to get you in a place of readiness to receive the greater, bigger, and better blessing. Greater is what God wants for His children; His word tells us so. The apostle Paul tells the church of Ephesus that God "is able to do exceedingly, abundantly above all we ask or think," which tells us whatever we ask of God—whatever we are thinking of—He is able, and He will answer in an exceedingly, abundant way. My God, that is good! It is wonderful to know God loves you enough to first, keep His promise and, second, to deliver in a way you did not know to speak of or think of. Pause and praise God right now for loving you enough not to give you what you asked for, but to give you what He has for you! I do not know about you, but I would much rather receive what God has for me than what I thought I would like for myself.

Reflecting on my cousin's prayer for furniture, by having a houseful of furniture, she was not only blocking her blessing without realizing it, but she was also blocking the blessings of her neighbors and others. Have you done the same thing? Have you blocked your blessings without realizing it? This happens because you want your blessings the way you want them to come to fruition, and you want them right now. No judgment, that is human nature. What you fail to realize is when you force your blessing in your timing, you are cheating yourself of the exceedingly abundantly above all that God has for you. You are also no longer in the perfect will and timing of God; instead, you are operating in His permissive will and timing.

The quickest way to mess ourselves up is by not waiting on God. Hear me! Waiting is a process to get us where God wants to bless us exceedingly and abundantly. Waiting is the time when God is preparing us for a greater blessing than what we asked for or thought about. Waiting in the preparation chamber or birthing room is where the rubber meets the road, and we are transformed into whom God has preordained us to be. Preparing until our something happens may not be, nor should it be, the most comfortable place, but it is well worth the prep work. Just like college students preparing for their graduation, so we prepare for our graduation. And with each class, there are lessons to be learned, work to be completed, and exams to be passed. Then there will be elevation. The harder the prep work, the longer the preparation, and the greater the blessing. And who does not want the greater blessing?

As my father says, "If you stay ready, you won't have to get ready." I am sure he did not coin that phrase, but he and my daughter Sydney are the only people I know who live by it. I believe five of the ten virgins had that same thought process. They stayed prepared for the bridegroom while the other five missed their blessing. Stay alert, keep your wicks trimmed and oil plentiful, and do not miss your blessing by not being prepared. Preparation is the key to getting ahead.

How do you prepare yourself? "Be diligent to present yourself approved to God" (2 Timothy 2:15). Here are a few steps to prepare yourself:

- Study the word of God for yourself.
- Develop a consistent, persistent, and deliberate praying life.
- Live according to the scriptures.

God has good and perfect gifts for His children for which He has prepared you. His gifts are so good and perfect that seeing them in you will cause others in your vicinity to stop and shout, "Nobody but God could do a thing like that!" All His good and perfect gifts are in a preparation cycle, which God will prepare you for despite what the situation looks like and what every naysayer is speaking. God has prepared you for greater. God has prepared you for the overflow. God has prepared you for exceedingly abundantly above all you asked or thought.

The more and more you allow God to prepare you, the more and more the preparation process becomes easier. When you consider what you are asking of God, or what God has called you to do, it is far easier to go through the preparation with God on your side than the alternative—to rush through life without Him. There is no reward for disobedience; rebellion gets us nowhere fast. Disobedience to God can cause you to spiral into the abyss while you are trying to make your own will happen. A child of God doing his own thing apart from God is a child of God who is completely out of order.

The Gospel of Matthew tells us, "But seek first the kingdom of God and His righteousness, and all these things shall be added to you" (Matthew 6:33). Allow me to add this sidenote: it was recently brought to my attention that in contractual contexts "shall" means "without negotiation and compromise." Believe it or not, Matthew 6:33 is a contractual agreement. How powerful to know that if you seek God first, everything you need (according to the previous verses) shall be yours and shall be yours without negotiation or compromise.

In Matthew chapter 6, Jesus says three times, "Do not worry." And yet worry happens. I am not saying you should not be concerned about troubling things, but worry is a direct negative reflection of your faith in God. Did you know you have measures of faith? You can reach a level of faith to get you where you could only imagine healing for a loved one's body, purchasing a new home, or getting a promotion on your job. With each level of your faith, there is preparation necessary. The preparation to receive His blessings without negotiation or compromise is to have faith in Him and Him alone.

Often, I pray that God would stretch my faith to believe Him for what seems impossible, stretch my faith to believe Him for unprecedented favor, or stretch my faith to participate in the miracles He has for others. I am asking of God to allow me to experience what is beyond comprehension. But let me warn you, that is a hard prayer to pray and even harder to believe. When God breathes on His blessings, He gives life to the His blessing. John 10:10 says, "I have come that they may have life and that they may have it more abundantly." How blessed it is to know that your faith coupled with God's abundance will produce miracles that will see you through the toughest of tough times.

So. answer this question: how much faith will it take to get God's attention? The correct answer is mustard-seed faith, but you must put that mustard-seed faith to work. After all, your faith does have feet. What you are asking of God requires unwavering faith, stretched faith, and a strong and straight posture of faith and faithfulness. Hebrews 11:1 gives us the clearest definition of faith: "NOW FAITH is the assurance (the confirmation, the title deed) of the things [we] hope for, being the proof of things [we] do not see and the conviction of their reality [faith perceiving as real fact what is not revealed to the senses] (AMP).[2]

You are probably thinking *Faith is work, and faith is hard.* You are correct again. However, consider how Jesus reprimanded His disciples when they displayed disbelief. What He said of them He says of us, "Oh ye of little faith." We see that we offend God by not trusting or believing in Him in every aspect of our lives.

Over my decades on this planet, I have learned that if God spoke it, He will bring it to pass. He cannot and will not lie. He is a rewarder of them who diligently seek Him, and He will never leave us, nor forsake us. Those are just a few of His promises, but that is all I need, just a few.

What about you? How many promises of God do you need before you completely trust Him, believe Him, and have faith in Him?

---

[2] The Amplified Bible. Copyright ©1954, 1958, 1962, 1964, 1965, 1987 by The Lockman Foundation. All rights reserved. Used by permission. Published by Zondervan. Grand Rapids, Michigan 49530, U.S.A.

DAWN L. CRUMBLE

Chapter 9
Pursue God

Follow closely. Run after. Chase down. To be determined with intensity, and diligent in your pursuit. Yes, that is exactly what happens when you are pursued, or when you pursue. You can pursue whatever and whomever your heart desires, whenever and wherever you are moved to do so. You have prayed the prayer of faith, believing, and trusting in God for His divine intervention in your situation. Now what? In your relentless pursuit of God's promises, there comes a time when you may feel overwhelmed, frustrated, alone, and desperate. I say to you, do not give up! In the pursuit, there will come a time when your immediate and prominent focus will be on the promise and not the promise-maker. And that is natural. You want the promise, and the keeper of the promise wants you to have the promise. While you are waiting on the manifestation of your already answered prayer, be compelled to focus on the promise-keeper.

Throughout the Holy Scriptures, the multitudes pursued (followed) Jesus intentionally and with a passionate purpose. Whether the multitude's pursuit was for healing in their bodies or deliverance from demons, or even to get a glimpse of Him, they would not be denied their goal. The blind beggar inquired of the multitude as he could hear the chatter of His arrival. Jesus' arrival has sound, and the blind beggar heard Jesus passing by. With his blind self, just hearing that Jesus was soon to pass him, he pursued Jesus, crying out, "Jesus, Son of David, have mercy on me."

Even with the consistent discouragement from the crowd, he was unbothered and continued with his relentless pursuit of the Savior. I love his attitude of "I do not care; I want what I want, and I will not quiet down!" Because of the blind man's faith and his determination, he received his sight. In this instance, Jesus asked him, "What do you want Me to do for you?" Jesus assured him, "Go your way; your faith has made you well." Be sure in your pursuit of Jesus, when He arrives and asks, "What do you want Me to do for you?" that you will answer precisely, so He can do for you according to your faith.

Consider Zacchaeus. He climbed the sycamore tree just to see Jesus. And as it turned out, Jesus was coming to stay at his house. Zacchaeus was in resolute pursuit of the Savior. That is the exact way you must pursue the promise-keeper—without hesitation, without delay, without intimidation, and unafraid. In your pursuit of what God has promised, your pursuit of Him should be with such intense laser focus that you begin to imitate Him, look like Him, and sound like Him. Will focusing on the promise get you closer to the promise? Or will focusing on the promised deliverer get you closer? I prefer the latter. In time, people will be drawn to your character, not because of who you are, but because of whose you are. Selah!

In the Gospel of Mark, Chapter 1, verse 36, Simon and the others searched for Jesus. When they searched for Him, they were not just looking for Him physically, but their earnest search was for His character to be able to examine Jesus with concentration. They wanted a closer relationship with Him to learn from and of Him and emulate Him. This type of pursuit is for more than any promise or answered prayer. This pursuit is for a closer relationship with your Savior. While you are waiting for the manifestation of God's already-answered prayer, what are you pursuing? Are you pursuing the promise of the prayer or the One who can and will deliver on His promise? How long are you willing to stay in the pursuit? And at what cost? I am confident your pursuit of God, Jesus, and Holy Spirit will be life-changing, not only for you but for those watching near and far.

When you think of what you are passionate about, how long will you wait for that new handbag you cannot do without, or the job promotion, or that newfound love relationship—how long will you wait? You pursue your passions with everything in you. You set aside time to talk and prepare yourself at a moment's notice to spend intimate time. Well, guess what? God wants the same with you. He longs to be pursued by you with everything you have within your heart, soul, and mind. He desires a closer relationship with you. Do you desire a closer relationship with Him? Your pursuit should not be surface only and convenient for you. Your pursuit must be consistent and insistent.

Your consistent pursuit of God happens daily and when you do not feel like it. You are consistent when others do not understand. Consistent when pursuing Him is at 5:00AM. Consistency is power, and there is power in His presence.

The word "insistent" is an adjective meaning "insisting or demanding something; not allowing refusal." What a WOW statement—not allowing refusal. This reminds me of Jacob when he wrestled with God. God had made Jacob a promise to bless him. In Jacob's pursuit of God, it is without a doubt that this conversation with God became Jacob's moment of not allowing refusal. He refused to let God go without receiving the promised blessing. A spirit of insistent determination had come over Jacob and that is exactly how you should be in your pursuit of the promised blessing. You cannot afford to throw in the towel with delays, loneliness, or impending devastation. When God speaks the promised blessing, He will not take it back, He will not deny it, and He will not cause you any sorrow. God stands strong on His promises. "His blessing makes one rich, and He adds no sorrow with it" (Proverbs 10:22).

Why prolong any further? Pursue God for His promised blessing. Pursue Him with all your heart, with all your determination, and with all your diligence. The wrestling may be hard and uncomfortable, but the promise is worth the fight. Are you ready to get into the fight of your life? The fight of your life may sound overwhelming and a bit intimidating but remember the promise of God in Isaiah 43:2, "When you pass through the waters, I will be with you; and through the rivers, they shall not overflow you. When you walk through the fire, you shall not be burned, nor shall the flame scorch you." WOW! What a promise.

Not only does God promise to be with you, but what you will go through will not overflow or overwhelm you. Now here is the cherry on top. You will not look like what you have been through. Remember this: it is much easier going through the hard times with God than without God. I have learned that when God makes a promise, He will see you through, provide for the promise, and be with you every step of the way. Coming out of the going through now looks better than before.

It is okay to go through because God has already been where He is taking you. Go ahead and go through but do it consistently and insistently. I will be sure to look for you on the other side of the going-through. There is something great ahead of you. Do not dare look back. Keep pursuing and do not let God go until He blesses you with what He promised.

DAWN L. CRUMBLE

Chapter 10
Plan for Greater

Has God given you an idea, vision, or plan and you have wondered, *how in the world can I do that?* Do not worry. If it is God's plan, He will do the instructing and give insight, clarity, discernment, know-how, and the resources to get it done.

Thinking back to March 2015 to be exact, God asked me, "What do you want me to do?"

I love when God asks me what I want Him to do for me. It makes me feel special. However, at that moment, I did not have an easy answer. I responded, "I want to have a prayer breakfast."

God's response was quick. "You can do a prayer breakfast all day long in your sleep. What do you want me to do for you?"

I had to think. "I want to host a prayer conference."

Again, God's answer was as if He had shrugged

His shoulders. "Okay, you can do that."

One more time God asked, "What do you want from *Me*?" I imagine God getting frustrated with me because there was something He saw in me, and I was either afraid to ask or I was not seeing my potential.

By this third time around, I realized what I was asking for was too small. God had something so big in mind for me, that to pull it off would take Him to do it and I would just be along for the ride. This truth finally clicked in my spirit (another ah-ha moment). "I want to host a city-wide prayer rally on the steps of the California State Capitol!"

And just like that, God answered, and I felt His smile. "Now you are talking!"

With anxious satisfaction, I reflected. "WOW, what did I just tell God I wanted?" I was no longer in a rush to experience what God would do in me, through me, for me, with me, or by me. With an assignment of that magnitude comes much greater responsibility. This would be huge. I then knew for sure this request was well beyond my capability without God. I would need God like never before.

Now it's your turn. Ask God for something grand, something on a scale bigger than yourself, something others are not doing, and you want to be the first to pull off.

At the time of the conversation with God about the city-wide prayer rally on the steps of the state capitol, *Women Who Pray* had not even had a prayer call yet. But here I was asking God for something beyond my ability, beyond my understanding, and beyond me. I had no choice but to wait and seek Him for direction. Most importantly, I waited for His timing.

Over the course of five years, every morning at 5:00AM, God's plan was coming together, and I had no clue He was truly working in my favor behind the scenes. The realization did not hit me until June 2019 when Pastor Tony Stewart of CityLife Church visited New Season Church in Sacramento. He asked me one question. "Are you willing to go to the edge of where God has never taken you before?" He then declared over my life, "Now is the time, this is the place, and you are the one."

Immediately, God spoke in my spirit. "Set the date for the capitol prayer rally."

It had just gotten real; God was setting His vision in motion, and I was part of it. In moments like this, you depend solely on God. It is the only way you will survive and thrive.

In March 2020, the world would experience a pandemic that ultimately would kill millions, causing nations to close all means of international travel. The Centers for Disease Control and other international health organizations were working around the clock to find the cause and a cure of the COVID-19 plague. As people panicked, a frenzy descended on the nation for toilet paper and hand sanitizer.

Why God? What is going on in the spirit realm that we are not seeing?" I wondered.

The very next day, God saw fit that a document answering my question about the coronavirus was placed in my desk inbox. The document was titled "Dismantling the Spirits Behind the Coronavirus." As I read, I remember thinking, *My God in Heaven!*

This explained so much. I was reading words such as panic, confusion, infirmity, hoarding, deception, insecurity, control, poverty, chaos, division, isolation, and fear.

My immediate curiosity wondered, *Where did this document come from? How did it get into my inbox?* No one in our office confessed to putting it in my desk tray, but it certainly explained everything that the world was facing. We were in a pandemic for certain. Those twelve words I had read were spirits and they suddenly made sense of the spiritual and natural realms.

Now, what was I to do with this information? It was too good and too important to keep to myself. I was instructed by God to call twelve preachers together for a twelve-night revival to dismantle those twelve spirits. That is exactly what I did. It was one of the hardest assignments ever, but I pressed onward into the presence of God like never before. Challenging events rose up during the planning. One preacher canceled the day of his assignment, and the livestream was demon-possessed, yet I pressed on.

The revival turned out to be a blessed and powerful twelve nights. My adrenaline was on 1,000. I thought it was me. Was I too excited? Then the word of the Lord came to me through Apostle Sam Wagner, "Woman of God, you are to dismantle quarterly!" The 12-Night Dismantling Revival went on once a quarter for the remainder of 2020. Twelve preachers, twelve nights, dismantled twelve spirits.

On December twelfth, we were scheduled to hold the capitol prayer rally that God and I talked about five years earlier. With rumors of impending rioting, the capitol security (aka the California Highway Patrol) expressed their concern for our safety, and they canceled our rally. Disappointed for about thirty seconds, I then turned to the Father. "God, what do I do now?" When you are available and following His plan, He will work it out better than you can imagine. It is His promise to work "exceedingly abundantly above all you ask or imagine."

That is exactly what He did. "Move the rally to Livestream." That was God's instruction. Just like that, the worship leader and every speaker were able to adjust, and we were able to minister to thousands of souls across the nation and around the world, instead of the one hundred we were allowed in prison. It was exceedingly abundantly above all I asked or thought! I watched God's plan come to fruition as He had ordained before the foundation of the world.

That is what will happen when you follow God's plan and do not try to get God to follow your plan. Your plans cannot and will not work without God. For this reason alone, it is imperative that you follow Him. Get aboard with Him and do it quickly. Think about the many times Jesus instructed His disciples to get in the boat, wait here, or go to the other side. There is no real plan if it is not God's plan. Remember, the word God gave Jeremiah. "For I know the thoughts that I think toward you, says the Lord, thoughts of peace and not of evil, to give you a future and a hope." With this promise of certainty, what plan has God given to you? When God gives you His plan, be sure you also know when to move, where to go, who needs to go with you, or who will be impacted. It is not important to know why. Just follow Him.

Planning has a deliberate purpose and requires your participation. Sure, you can sit back and expect miracles from Heaven, but I am reminded of two pointers from Deuteronomy 28:1-2:

1. Diligently obey the voice of God.
2. Observe carefully all His commandments.

Obeying His voice and observing all His commandments is your way of being attentive and mindful of every detail of His plan for you. This is another reason why I journal to make sure I get every detail. I recommend you do the same. The same way we are to "seek first the Kingdom of God and His righteousness" (Matthew 6:33) is the same way He will provide everything we need for His plan. We must be attentive to His vision, His will, and His purpose. When we are attentive to His plan, He will be attentive to us.

God's plan for you is much greater than your plan for yourself, and it will succeed, but you must be willing to follow. Do not be afraid of His plan. God's plan probably does not resemble your plan, but when you gave God your *yes*, your *yes* indicated your submission and willingness to be used. The plan will work; it is God's plan and God's plans always work. Are you ready for His plan to impact your life?

Chapter 11
Position Yourself

Have you considered your position until something happens? What position are you in to receive the promises of God? Do you like your position? Do others like you in your position? Is it a position of wealth, stagnation, jealousy, bitterness, pride, or fear? Whatever your position, God has an intentional place for you with your name on it. Position or status comes with responsibility, should look like humility, and is wearable to the most unlikely. Are you in the position God has created for you? For where God is taking you? For whom you will impact? Standing, sitting, and laying are all positions that God can use for His glory and the good of others. Let's get into the labor position until your something happens.

Position yourself for vision and birthing. A series on Netflix caught my attention. *Call the Midwife* is a series about midwives and midwife-

Nuns is set in the late 1800s through the mid-1900s in Poplar, England. They reside together in the worn-down convent but have birthed generations in that small town. The midwives assisted the mother from possibly their third trimester through the moment of cutting the newborn's umbilical cord. Rarely was a doctor required for birth because the midwives were experts in every possible birthing scenario and position.

What grabbed me was how the midwives had the foreknowledge of what they could physically diagnose during appointments. They also could coach and direct the mother into the inevitable push. They even handled the supporting family members—the nervous father, the know-it-all mother, and the bothersome other children. With each anxious mother-to-be, the midwife could facilitate the birthing process with the calm of her voice, the assuredness of her strength, and the certainty that she was not new at this.

The midwife repeats these commands, "Breathe slowly. Now, short pants. Turn on your side. Get on your knees. Push. I can see the head. Push. The shoulders are out. One more really good PUSH! And we are there."

These midwives were skilled experts and controlled the most impossible situation. Some things were unforeseen to the moms, but the midwives had the foresight to prepare for the worst case, make adjustments for mom and baby, and have a contingency plan to turn to if necessary. They could detect premature births, breech births, and false labor.

This all may seem normal for midwives, but I soon realized their actions sound like the work of Holy Spirit. Just like the midwives, Holy Spirit is with you to guide and direct you through the birthing process of the vision with which God has impregnated you.

With every vision God plants within you, there must be a plan and a midwife. The plan is your target, and your midwife will help you hit your target. It is time you identify your midwives; they will need to understand God's plan and vision for you. Your midwives are your greatest supporters and must be in alignment with the vision. Listen to your midwives; their job is not the easiest, but it is very necessary. They will know when it is time for you to get into position to breathe, when to pant, when to shift, and definitely when to push. Though the vision may seem like it is taking longer than expected, the baby will surely come. Do not be surprised if your midwives are not who you expected or wanted. God will give you specific midwives for every plan. And often they know the plan before God gives you the vision.

I have several midwives. I listen attentively to their instructions, and I take notes. I clearly remember when God said, "Start a prayer ministry," and while I believed I knew how to pray, I asked God for a mentor (my midwife). God gave me two mentors, and they came in the persons of Evangelist Yvonne Gibson Johnson and Pastor Stephanie Douglas. Anointed and skilled in the ministry of intercessory prayer, Evangelist Johnson gave me one instruction. "Read *Draw the Circle* by Mark Batterson." The subtitle of the book is *The 40 Day*

Prayer Challenge. I did not want a challenge. I did not need a challenge. I knew how to intercede, pray, fast, and petition God, or so I thought.

Pastor Stephanie coached and instructed me through developing the dos and don'ts of the morning prayer call. During my year-long pregnancy, they were my midwives: coaching, correcting, encouraging, keeping me focused, and walking with me through crazy times and hard seasons. At the first anniversary of *Women Who Pray Ministries*, Pastor Stephanie preached for my first prayer breakfast which was a huge success. I had birthed the first of many babies who would be born from the ministry of *Women Who Pray*.

I know my midwives intimately and consider them wise women of God. I did not always want to listen, but it was for my best that I did. My midwives helped me get to where I am now, and they continue to help me.

God would soon impregnate me again with visions of international ministry expansion, an academy for girls, live broadcasting, and a series of books. I am pregnant with quadruplets. With each vision, my midwives are still present, some new to ease the load and to continue pouring into me. I am in the fetal position, pushing, breathing, and panting, but soon the scream and sigh of deliverance will be mine to share with the nations.

What are you pregnant with? Is your vision one of continuing your education, starting a business, starting a ministry, or changing careers? Have you been pregnant and did not know what to do? Or were you pregnant and did not realize it until midpregnancy? During this impregnation, sometimes nine months, but sometimes much longer, God begins to bring His vision into the light of our spirit. Each vision comes with its gestation period. None is the same, very much like when we birth our natural children, no pregnancy is the same. You should not expect God's vision to be the same as others' either. When God gives you His vision, His plan, it may not always be as clear as you would like. Still, you know there is something in you that must be birthed: birthed to bless others, birthed to bring greatness to the world, birthed in brilliance. God has not impregnated you with junk, but rather with an absolute fortune. What kind of fortune are you carrying?

Another position I would like to share with you is the position of a diligent seeker. The writer of Hebrews 11:6 says, "But without faith it is impossible to please Him, for he who comes to God must believe that He is, and that He is a rewarder of those who diligently seek Him." To win, you must position yourself to become a diligent seeker of God. It takes faith to seek God diligently. It takes faith to please God. It takes faith to obey and follow God. It takes faith to believe in God when all catastrophic chaos is looming around us. It takes faith!

Our seeking cannot be a once-in-a-while seeking. We must seek Him daily and relentlessly, without wavering or hesitation. Say this out loud, "I cannot please God without faith in Him." Now repeat this out loud: "Because I am coming to God, I must believe He is my rewarder because I am diligently seeking Him." Why out loud? Because your verbal expression does three things:

1. It will encourage you.
2. It will strengthen those around you, and
3. It will serve notice on the enemy that you solely and earnestly have faith in God.

What does seeking God have to do with us being in or getting into position? Positioning yourself to diligently seek God assures you that you are in the presence of the One who will be your rewarder. Every time you position yourself to do the will of God, you are deliberately placing yourself within the reach of His blessing path. You have prayed for this, that, and the other, all while seeking God diligently for His direction, His strength, and His clarity. You may not feel as if you are getting anywhere in the process, but rest assured, God sees your every move, collects your every tear, and knows your every thought.

What better position could you be in? God will position you for His reward, and His reward cannot be compared to any other. God will deliberately allow you to go through a troubling situation to get you into your designated position. The position has authority. The position has grace. The position has structure. The position will break you, equip you, and fortify you all at the same time. Seek the rewarder like your life depends on it. As you seek Him, your faith will be stretched, and pleasing God will become easier. When your ways please the Lord, He will make even your enemies be at peace with you. (Proverbs 16:7) The result is you will be in a better position than you were without a loving Father.

What are you seeking God for? It may be too hard for you to fully grasp and comprehend, but God knows exactly where your faith level is and what you need to shift your faith into gear. I am reminded of when I began to feel God pulling me away from my job at Sacramento State. I remember resting on the wall in Tahoe Hall and saying, "God, it feels like you are moving me into full-time ministry, and I am okay with that. But, if you give me three more years, I will be vested and will not have to worry about the girls."

In His sovereignty, God replied, "I can give you the three years, but my benefits are better than the State of California's."

Immediately my faith shifted into overdrive and my answer was and still is, "Well, Lord, let's go with your plan." I found out that day my faith level was catapulted to a place where only my pleasing God would take me. Five months later, my job with the university ended, and I have not looked back. In fact, I lived better than I did with a man-made job. How is that for radical, God-pleasing faith?

Let God stretch your faith to believe Him for the impossible, the uncommon, the irregular, and the unusual. God is not basic, and your faith should not be either. My strong suggestion to you is to have faith in God. He knows what is best for you.

Chapter 12
Pour and Be Poured Into

To those who have come across her remarkable story in 2 Kings 4:1-7, she is known as the Widow Woman. She's unnamed (but feel free to insert your name here if you have ever been in a desperate situation), and she knows a few things:

1. She recognized the prophet of God and cried out for help.
2. She knew to follow God's instructions.
3. She knew (whether she realized it or not) that following God's instructions would give her the answer she desperately sought Him for.

Her place of desperation came from the news that her husband's creditor was coming for her two sons to be slaves as repayment for his debt. Much like the sentiment of any modern-day parent, your sons (or daughters) becoming slaves under your watch was not happening as long as there was breath in your body. Can you relate to her desperate cry? Can you imagine someone coming after your child as repayment for a debt that you nor they had any control over and most likely did not know anything about? Absolutely not. Not today, not tomorrow, not ever!

Doing the only thing that could be done, she cried out to Elisha the prophet. Some may question, why cry out to a man and not God for herself? Let me assure you, there will be times when you will need the counsel of men, but the counsel will be God-led and God-ordained. She went to the man of God to receive the word, instructions, or affirmations she could trust because they would be delivered by and through God's servant. In her desperate moment, God sent His word through the prophet. This Widow Woman was asked two questions:

"What shall I do for you? and

"What do you have in the house?"

She neglected to answer the first question; however, she did not hesitate to answer the second. She never told Elisha what she wanted. Could it have been obvious? Could it have been crystal clear? Could it have been the same response you would have given? Looking over everything in her house, she replied with what I imagine was some hesitation. "Your maidservant has nothing in the house but a jar of oil."

While she may have concluded that oil was all she had, the oil had significance and wealth tied to it. When was the last time you cried out to God? She knew there was one creditor and what his plan was. She knew she had nothing in the house but one jar of oil. What's in your house that you have overlooked or did not recognize as significant? Are there vessels at your disposal that you have pushed aside? She was concerned about her sons. She had no intention of allowing the creditor to win at his plan. She was desperate for whatever would keep her sons from enslavement and desperate for whoever could get the job done. She did what desperate moms do, she listened, and she availed herself.

She was given five to-dos. "Go, borrow, shut the door, pour, and set aside." In her anguish, she obeyed the word, all I's dotted, and every T crossed. She went and borrowed as many vessels as her neighbors had. She shut the door behind her and her sons. She poured the oil until she had no more empty vessels to fill, and then she set the full vessels aside.

The prophet Elisha then gave her four more to-dos. "Go, sell, pay, and live." And just like that, she and her sons immediately became the recipients of a lifetime blessing. This is what an act of desperate obedience will get you: a lifetime of blessings, a continual overflow, and perpetual benefits. One act of obedience and now she is a business owner.

What happened to her can also happen to you. Are you the next multi-millionaire business owner? Are you next? Maybe your sons are not being chased down to be slaves, you may not have to borrow actual vessels, and you may not have to pour oil, but one thing I know is as her life happened, so will yours.

Let me put it in layman's terms. You find yourself in a pickle, you seek the counsel of your pastor, and he or she gives you instructions. Now, these instructions may supernaturally sound like, "Go minister to someone or share your testimony, shut the door, and spend some time with Me (says the Lord). Pour into the life of someone who is on the brink of suicide or set aside that plate for a period of fasting." What dead situation in your now is affecting your future?

Pouring until something happens is another way of understanding desperate determination. Being desperate and determined will make you do anything and everything to save your children, your livelihood, and your integrity. Have you been pushed until your back is against the wall? Are you crying out for help with nowhere to go? You may feel defeated with no place for refuge and overwhelmed to the point of sheer madness. Who has not been there, crying out for deliverance while others look on wondering, "Where is her help"?

The Widow Woman was desperate enough to follow the instructions given by the prophet Elisha. It is time for you to get desperate enough to cry out! Here is a bonus for you: It is perfectly okay to get others involved in your recovery, your deliverance, and your healing. I know people who have cut off their blessings out of fear of what others will think. When you get desperate enough, you will not care what others think.

This Widow Woman poured the oil until she had filled the borrowed vessels. Could you be the vessel God is looking to pour into? Or are you the one who is supposed to be pouring into someone else's life, but you're afraid to get involved? Whichever person you are, they both require humility and strength. Make yourself available for the oil of God. It is powerful, it is life-changing, and it is necessary.

Considering all that God is capable of, it would behoove you to follow God desperately and know with great confidence that He is able to do exceedingly, abundantly, above all you ask or imagine according to the power that works in us (Ephesians 3:20). God has something for you above what you are asking or thinking. Just when you thought you were heading down the road of defeat, the road of losing everything, the road of sickness and disease, the road of poverty, the road of divorce, and the road of prodigal children, God sends instructions. Are you listening? Have you missed the instructions? Are you ready? It is time for you to throw all caution to the wind, forget what it looks like, turn a deaf ear to every naysayer, and follow God with desperate determination. What is in your future that requires you to separate yourself from what is common, what is regular, what is basic, and what is usual? What God has for you is above all!

There is a lifetime blessing waiting on you, and it is all dependent upon your obedience. Let me suggest that you not miss your lifetime blessing because of your disobedience. God has miracles for you that will not only change your life but will also change the lives of those around you. This woman (do not forget to insert your name here) did a few things to get what she desperately needed, even though she did not fully know what it was she needed. Her concern was for her sons. The remedy to her desperation took care of more than her sons. Her obedience and desperation ushered her into a lifetime of blessing, and the oil flowed to the overflow.

That is exactly what I want, overflow! How about you? I am sure you could use an overflow of the blessings of God in your life. This is what I call cause and effect. The cause was to save her sons from becoming slaves. The effect was to get the creditor paid in full and the extended miracle, her lifetime residual blessing. She received beyond what she was expecting. That is just how God does us. He provides exceedingly, abundantly, above all we ask or think. The end result is a lifetime of residual blessings.

Let me set the course of experiencing and participating in miracles. Have you ever received instructions from the Lord that may sound crazy, outlandish, or impossible to achieve, but you obey simply because you are desperate, and your back is up against the wall? I suggest to you, be willing to put in the work for the blessing. Just like you need God to perform the miracle, God needs you to obey His instructions and put boots to the ground for the miracle.

As much as we would like to surmise that miracles and blessings fall out of the sky, they are not free! Miracles and blessings come with a cost. Are you ready to pay the cost? Or as one of my favorite authors would say, "Are you ready to pray the cost?" The cost is obeying God even when it does not feel good, look good, or sound good. The cost is obeying God when it is not popular, convenient, or easy. Sometimes the cost is the purging of friends, family, and foes. The cost can be time spent in the hard places.

Whatever the cost, are you ready? I hear some of you sitting there saying to yourself, "Why is there a cost on my obedience?"

My friend, there was also a cost to Jesus' obedience. I will ask you again, no, rather let me stress to you, let's get ready for the cost. This is how you become the Second Kings Widow Woman, or let's change her (your) name to the Second Kings Winning Woman (or man). It is time for us to "Go, sell, pay, and live" all for the glory of God!

DAWN L. CRUMBLE

Chapter 13
Pause and Please

Pause: to interrupt or temporarily stop an action. What needs to be paused in your life? Do you have too many distractions, hindrances, and weights that are not yours to carry? Let's pause for a moment to hear the voice of God. What does it mean to pause your life to pray? It does not mean to stop living and taking care of business. It does mean pausing long enough to hear from God. It means use your discernment and don't miss any instructions. It means your season of waiting is close to an end, but you must pause, and in your pausing, the vision, plan, and purpose will become clearer. Pause temporarily to refocus on what God has shown you. Allow God's interruptions and temporary stops in life to direct you. Do not try to direct Him or them. Pausing prayer is not a permanent stop; it is a time to be still and a place of refreshing where you allow yourself to be vulnerable.

Let's pause to hear from God. What is God saying to you in this season?

Recently, God spoke these words to me: "It is time to experience the WOWs I have for you."

As I began thinking about all God had done for me this year, every moment was a wow. Wow with a new job. Wow with my first international ministry trip to the United Kingdom. Wow with the purchase of my first home. And absolutely wow with this book deal. Of course, there were other wows, some big and others small, but yet they were God wows, and I could not have experienced miracle after miracle without Him orchestrating the moments, the open doors that were on purpose, deliberate, and had my name attached to them. Just wow, God!

As I think about it now, my wow moments with God began at the exact moment I said yes to Him in 1989 and again in 2015. As I see it, every moment God has blessed me with, every moment I have spent with Him, and every moment He has used me to bless others are all wow moments.

Preceding every wow was a pause to hear from and to remember His promises. Remembering His promises taught me that His promises for me are yes in Him and amen in Him, not me. Yes in Him says He does not go back on His word. Amen in Him says He has settled it, and it is so. At this moment, I am more appreciative of God's interruptions of my plans, His temporary stops to my opportunities, and His moments telling me, "Just wait and see what I have for you." And you will be abundantly appreciative too. Just sit back and accept God's wows; the good, the bad, and the ugly—all of them.

Wows come in good, great, hard, bad, and not so bad. Just because a wow moment is difficult, hard, or even bad, that does not mean they are not from God. We can learn better and hear more clearly in the difficult, hard, and bad wows too. They offer some of the most powerful and life-transforming experiences. Negative wow moments can also change the course of someone else's life for generations to come. Wow moments are also revelatory. They give insight, knowledge, and wisdom. James 1:5 tells us, "If any of you lacks wisdom, let him ask of God, who gives to all liberally and without reproach, and will be given to him."

The Greek translation for wisdom is the word "sophia." Sophia means "in respect to divine things, wisdom, knowledge, insight, deep understanding, represented everywhere as a divine gift and including the idea of practical application." Sophia stands for divine wisdom, the ability to regulate one's relationship with God" (James 1:5).[3]

In WOW moments with God, use sophia (wisdom). God will give you sophia liberally for that moment in that season. A different level of sophia is designed for every pause and interruption. Sophia is required and will get you through the level of wows you will experience, whether good, great, hard, or bad. I always believed wisdom was a woman.

Another pause is to wait or tarry. As the prophet Habakkuk puts it (and I'm giving it my spin), even when God's vision seems to be taking forever, His timing is in play—not yours, and you must wait for

---

[3]*Hebrew-Greek Key Word Study Bible* NKJV, AMG, 2015, pg 2555, #4678

it. You will get the manifestation of your vision when God says you are ready for it and not a minute sooner. After all, God still knows what is best for you, what you can handle, and how much of it you can handle. He gave you His vision, now wait, because when the blessing is released, the timing will be perfect, and you will be able to handle it. Just like when Jesus ascended, He told the disciples to wait for the promised gift. So just wait as the disciples did, for the promised gift will surely come.

What Do You Need to Pause?

_____
_____
_____
_____
_____
_____
_____
_____
_____
_____
_____

What Do You Need to Wait For?

_____
_____
_____
_____
_____
_____
_____
_____

Chapter 14
Persist

When I think of a determined, persistent pursuit, getting what God has promised, I immediately think of my favorite scripture, Hebrews 11:6. "But without faith it is impossible to please Him, for he who comes to God must believe that He is, and that He is a rewarder of those who diligently seek Him." To diligently seek God means to pursue with a passion so embedded in you that you will not give up or give in. There is intent about your seeking that will push you and scare those around you. Diligently seeking God is a constant posture that should remind you of the value of that which you are seeking from the Rewarder.

The eleventh chapter of Hebrews is our chapter of faith. In its words, we are encouraged with the hope of knowing many before us pursued the Rewarder and they had the faith to get them through. You are looking in from the outside declaring, "If

Abel, Enoch, Noah, Abraham, Sarah, and the others could do it, so can I." They went through what seemed to be hopeless and helpless situations as you too have gone through. You could possibly be there now, but hold on, you will be rewarded in and after seeking God, His promises, and His will for your life. When others do not believe, you persist in believing God for every promise. Persistence is what will give you the courage to get through. Persistent faith will get you through even when you do not realize you are getting through. There is a blessing on the other side of the get-through.

My favorite scripture begins by saying, "But without faith…" To not have faith in God says you do not believe God can do it. You have asked, pleaded, begged, and asked again, but it seems like and feels like God has turned a deaf ear to you. Not true. What is your faith saying? Is your faith saying, "I will ask, but…" or is your faith saying, "He did it before, but I am not sure about this time," or is your faith saying, "God, I do not know how you will do it, but I trust you to get it done." What is your faith saying? Is your faith completely stretched to believe God for His promises, or is your faith resembling a limp noodle? You must decide to go to the edge of where God has never taken you. God has called you to something and because you have determined any or all of these, you stopped.

- I am not smart enough.
- I do not have the resources.
- No one will support me.
- I cannot do this.
- I will look foolish.

My Now is the time to move. Get up, dust yourself, your dreams, vision, purpose, and plans off, and move! Be persistent about God's business concerning you. If He is concerned, and the Bible says He is, move and obey His voice. What or who has kept you from moving, shifting, or pushing? Who or what has kept you from furthering your education, buying your first home, or starting your business? It is time to go to the edge of where God has never taken you. Do you believe God is the rewarder of those that diligently seek Him? Consider the list of five excuses above and confess the ones that have been keeping you from the edge where God wants to take you.

Edge - I Am Ready, Lord!

Going back to Hebrews 11:1, "Now, faith is the substance of things hoped for, the evidence of things not seen." Do you believe what God is showing you? Yes, it looks absolutely unattainable and seems even further away, but do you believe it? Listen, I grew up in a house and always wanted a house of my own once I became an adult. I wanted a place where my daughters would grow and call home. I convinced myself I would only be able to have a house by way of marriage. Then one day, I paid attention to God's promise of debt cancellation, and my credit was wiped clean as if the debt had never existed. Silly me, I could not figure it out. My daughter reminded me of God's promise.

Step one: my loan application was approved.

Step two: I went house shopping with my agent.

Step three: I signed my name countless times to close escrow.

If I'd stayed in that place of "I am stuck and I cannot get out," I would still be renting. It took persistent faith, stretched faith, crazy faith, and faith with feet to move when God said move. I was ready to go where God had never taken me before. And I dance every day I come home to my house.

In 2022, the baby of *Until Something Happens* had been birthed. God's vision began years before, but the germination process was taking longer than expected. I was anxious, and yet the Holy Scriptures tell us not to "be anxious for anything" (Philippians 4:6). At times I grew weary, and yet the Bible gives the command "and let us not grow weary" (Galatians 6:9). I began feeling discouraged, and yet God's Word encourages us. "I have come that they (you) may have life" (John 10:10). I had to come to the realization that God alone ordained *Until Something Happens,* and all I had to do was obey His commandments when I heard His voice. This part of the germinating season can be tough, but I learned it is only a season requiring persistent faith in God. There are four conditions necessary for germination.

Water - "He who believes in Me, as the Scripture has said, out of his heart will flow rivers of living water" (John 7:38). Where there is no living water, there is no life, and without life, persistence cannot and will not happen. The living water sustains by hydration and purifies your system to cleanse your pores, so you can pour into others. You need water as simple as it is, to live and to bring forth life. Just as with natural water to germinate various seeds for food, you need Christ, the living water to germinate various seeds of vision, purpose, plans, gifts, and goals that have been planted within you. Your seeds need water to germinate, to come into existence and develop. Wow, now that is revelatory!

It is time for you to come in from your stagnated posture in order to be who God has called you to be. It is time for you to develop into what God has ordained you to be. (Do not be tripped up by the word "ordained." Every minister is not in the pulpit.) I believe every Christian is called to a form of ministry. This is called ministry re-imagined (thank you, Midwife, Dr. Karen Gentry).

Are you existing in sub-standard spiritual conditions, unaware you need developing? Let's get you developed. Just like when there was a thing called "getting film developed" that took the negative film and turned it into a positive picture, it is the same with you. Development is in process and the solution to the matter is living water. What is God developing in you?

Oxygen - The ruach of God is the Spirit of God, the wind of God, and the breath of God.[4] The breath of God gives life. "Prophesy to the breath, prophesy, son of man, and say to the breath, "thus says the Lord God: Come from the four winds" (Ezekiel 37:9). In this instance, the ruach of God was present, giving life to the dead that they may live. The breath of God gives and restores life.

Just like with a plant, oxygen is as essential as water. They work together is ensure the growth and stability of the seed. A seed cannot take root without proper oxygen and the right environment.

An unusual encounter happened to me. God said, "Blow, and as you blow, I will breathe in you." I had never felt the breath of God before. In fact, I had never heard of anyone receiving the breath of God. I could feel the breath of God rushing through me. I expelled everything toxic with every breath. That was a cleansing that forever changed my life. The spirit of God gives you creativity, brings revival, and invigorates dry places. Do not allow your seed to be consumed in a dark, dry place. It needs water, oxygen, and light.

Light - "I am the light of the world. He who follows Me shall not walk in darkness but have the

---

[4] Hebrew-Greek Key Word Study Bible AMG, 2015. NKJV Pg. 2204, #7307

light of life" (John 8:12). Growth and stimulation are produced by light, and light is important to the germination process of the vision. Light brings revelation to the vision that will attract vision carriers to the purpose. When you follow the visionary, there is a personal light that will become so bright and luminous that the vision will be hard to miss. The light gives exponential growth to your light which cannot be turned off. A persistent relationship with the light strengthens you before, during, and after your germination season. The light will not dim, fade, or go out. The light will continue illuminating your life. As you follow the light of Christ, your light shines and those around you will witness to the power of the light.

Temperature - "So then, because you are lukewarm, and neither cold nor hot, I will vomit you out of My mouth" (Revelation 3:16). Your growth in the germination season requires persistent praying and fasting, daily devotion in Bible study, and honoring God with your tithes and offerings. Even with all this, the temperature must be right.

With thinner oxygen and less light, the colder temperature will slow down the growth process. Winter is for planning and nurturing. Hotter temperatures are preparing for the harvest. There is a distinct difference between the two seasons. Warm temperatures are indecisive and double-minded. Warm temperatures cannot decide if they are hot or cold. Do not be warm. God has not called you to be loopy in the head and being warm will only get you in trouble. Your vision will not have an iffy season, appear scatterbrained, or be confused. With the right temperature, the light, the breath of God, and the living water, your persistent demeanor will keep you until your something happens and will not fail you. Get ready for the shift, it is on its way says the Lord.

UNTIL SOMETHING HAPPENS

Until Next Time

Now that you have read my journey as an intercessor, you may be wondering what your "until something happens" looks like. I have come to realize that while God has already answered my prayers, I am waiting with supernatural expectation, patience, and endurance. I have realized there is a temporary process before I receive my permanent promise because there is so much to be done. I must be like Ezekiel and prophesy to the dry bones in my life. Ezekiel gave his situation the word of God (37:4). Praying effectively requires a knowledge of the holy scriptures. One thing for sure is God responds to His word.

While the wait may seem too long, the wait is worth it. What am I to do while waiting? I will praise and pray, just like Paul and Silas did in the book of Acts. I love that story because, like me on so many occasions, Paul and Silas were on their way to prayer when they encountered the young girl. On my way to prayer, I have been delayed many times. It always seemed like getting to prayer was a challenge, though I was determined to push my way there. While in those various times of delay, I never lost sight of my assignment. Some people were waiting on my arrival for prayer. They needed me as much as I needed them.

Prayer for me is my release, my place of sanctified strength, and my place of re-strengthening. I consider it a blessing to be called on to pray for and with someone. I often think it is too bad others do not find spiritual enjoyment in covering someone with prayer. While waiting on the manifestation of the already-answered prayer, I pray even more. I praise God even more and I prophesy to my dead, dry situations even more. Waiting can be hard, but I wait in the presence of the Almighty God, the one who knew me before I was formed in my mother's womb, the one who fashioned my days while I was yet unformed, and the One whose thoughts toward me are greater than the amount of sand on the earth. It makes me happy knowing God trusts me with His assignment.

What are you doing until your something happens? You have prayed and possibly even fasted. You may have marched around the situation like it was the city of Jericho, waiting for the walls to come tumbling down. You may have praised while in the fight to set up an ambush against your enemy. You may have been disappointed, and it seems like God is not answering. But be encouraged. God is preparing you for the bigger promise He has for you. We pray with a natural expectation and God answers exceedingly abundantly above all we ask or imagine.

Since we never ask or think big enough, God will always outdo what we think we want or what we think we need. That is why there are seasons of preparation and process. God must take time to prepare us for greater. And greater is what He will do.

Do not be afraid of the process. The process is temporary. At some point, the process will end, and you will have your promise. In most cases, the manifestation will not look like what you have prayed for; it will be better. Stop looking for God to answer your prayers according to your way and in your timing. God will always do you one better. He gives us what He wants us to have—His best.

I discovered that too. God gave me His best while I waited, prayed, prophesied, and did so much more. I did not abort the assignment, I kept praying. I did not throw my hands up as if God said no, I kept praising Him. I did not settle for less. I kept pressing into His presence. I did not forget His promises for me. I kept preparing, and I did not quit. I kept prophesying to my dead, dry situation just like Ezekiel prophesied to his.

The manifestation of the already-answered prayer was just an "until something happens" away. I kept believing God for being the Rewarder of those who diligently seek Him. And just like that, the manifestation of my already-answered prayer became a tangible reality.

About the Author

In 1989, Pastor Dawn Crumble humbly accepted the call and mantle of intercessory prayer on her life. Pastor Dawn once again said yes to God and in January 2015, Women Who Pray Ministries (WWPM), an ordained and consecrated ministry, came to fruition. WWPM stays true to its mission to serve hurting women coast to coast and border to border. As a result of this commitment, WWPM has grown from eight members to thousands and is represented in seventeen countries.

From the humble beginnings, Women Who Pray Ministries has become a tree of life for many with several ministry platforms led by Pastor Dawn and her team:

- 5 AM Prayer
- Prayer Intensifies New Knowledge Summit
- Dismantling the Spirits 12-Night Revival
- Friday Night Live

- Winning with my Sisters

With this mandate on Pastor Dawn's life, she endeavors to teach God's people about the ministry and gift of prayer through group events, teaching series, and prayer summits. Prayer is her passion, and she is called upon by many to intercede for pastors specifically. Pastor Dawn is a prayer and women's conference speaker, equipping church leaders and members in prayer.

Pastor Dawn currently attends Epic Bible College where she is studying to complete a Bachelor of Science degree in Biblical Counseling.

She is also the founder of Zion Girls Leadership and Collegiate Preparatory Academy; an academic and life skills academy for girls of incarcerated parents. Pastor Dawn Crumble lives in Sacramento, CA with her two daughters, Loren and Sydney.

www.ingramcontent.com/pod-product-compliance
Lightning Source LLC
Chambersburg PA
CBHW070429010526
44118CB00014B/1968